Our War

Buon Ho, Vietnam

1966-1967

**District staff and local leaders
Buon Ho, Vietnam 1966-1967**

Front cover:
Buon Ho District Headquarters compound

Rear Cover:
Sergeant Dian and friends
(The advisor's blue beret was Military Assistance Command Vietnam's idea)

ISBN 978-1-4357-0956-0

FORWARD

This is what occurred during a year's warfare on the Cambodian border in Buon Ho District, Darlac Province, Vietnam. Others may have a different recollection.

The quoted words are not verbatim but rather what is recalled as to the content and tenor used.

Some names have been changed.

Most was written after completing a second tour in Vietnam in 1969. Some comments are a result of that tour.

Getting There

CHAPTER ONE

After midnight the airport shuttle bus leaves Highway 101 and moves through the empty streets before stopping at Civic Center. Reflected light from City Hall's golden dome floods the area.

Two crew cut, weathered but well conditioned drunks, supporting each other, start up the steps as the bus door opens.

Sitting in the empty rear, I hear them yell at the driver "Travis?" It is the right bus—their looks tell you that.

Laughing, they turn, wave and shout good-bye. Two aging blondes clinging to a city trash can wave back. The men slide into the front seat, the door closes.

The bus starts up, speeds down Market, across the Bay Bridge, up Interstate 80 towards the valley and Sacramento.

At two that morning, an hour earlier then my travel orders require, it pulls into Travis Air Base air terminal's loading dock.

Walking into the terminal, I give my orders to the lone drowsy Air Force clerk in the vast barn like building. Looking at them he checks my name on a flight manifest, then tags and throws my duffel bag on the cart behind him.

"Take a seat sir, it'll be six hours till loading."

In the seating area khaki clad dozing teenage Army privates crowd the dark wooden pews, row after row, waiting for their flights.

I find a vacant spot, sit and open the Agatha Christie purchased at the Philadelphia airport when starting my trip.

These cheap, throwaway paperbacks are ideal for a flight, conveying you to a mind numbing, time passing, nonexistent world where English morality triumphs. Talking with the person sitting next to you will not disturb your reading since all stories are the same. And if read before you will not remember it.

"Hi," says Captain Chris Vurlumis as he walks up, right hand out.

We were Lieutenants together in an airborne battalion in Germany.

Our War

I hardly knew him, seeing him only in the mess hall or at mandatory battalion parties at the officer's club. His social life, as a bachelor assigned to a different company, was not the married officer's routine determined by our wives.

It surprises me that he is still in the Army. In the battalion a short time then gone, I heard he resigned. Slight of build and boyish looking, the rumor was that he did not fit and was run out of the battalion and the Army.

Now he stands before me, a big grin on his face, a large Japanese 35 mm camera draped around his neck. His left hand carries a black leather attaché—a tourist going on vacation. I shake hands with him as he sits down next to me.

Checking flight numbers confirms we are on the same plane.

The plane is a jetliner hired with its civilian crew from the commercial airlines that survive by leasing planes to Military Air Command. However, unlike commercial flights, seats are jammed in to hold as many bodies as possible.

When boarding is announced officers board first picking their seats before the several hundred privates crowd on. There are no assigned seats except for the plane commander, the senior officer on the flight, who sits next to the stewardesses, and the courier officer who sits at the exit, getting off first.

Vurlumis and I sit together, he wants a window seat, and talk. He babbles, telling me his life history; a native San Franciscan, an only son raised by his mother—while I read some more Christie mysteries—and sleep.

The plane lands at Ton Son Nhut twenty-four hours later, after pit stops in Hawaii, Midway and Okinawa. It is night. As we walk down the ramp heat and humidity rising from the tarmac engulfs us. Sweat soaks our khakis in the short walk across the tarmac to the hot, humid terminal.

There we are funneled into a fenced area.

Army finance clerks sit here in small wire mesh cages. They demand our American greenbacks; no American dollars are allowed in country. We exchange them

8

Getting There

for dollar script or Vietnamese dong. The script, colored paper printed to show an equal amount of dollars, are used to buy American beer or low cost Japanese Seiko watches or Sony stereos at Army Post Exchanges (PX). The Vietnamese Dong called Piasters or "P's" are needed to buy anything from the Vietnamese from having laundry done to getting a haircut or whatever.

The finance clerks zealously perform their task despite the heat. No greenback escapes them. They are stuffing Swiss bank accounts from profits made by buying script and Dong at a discount on the black market then selling them at the official rate to the newly arriving "grunts."

Vietnamese, slightly built muscular little men, unload and bring our baggage into the terminal as we make the exchange.

Army Non-Commissioned Officers (NCOs) then separate us based on our assigned unit.

Vurlumis is going to the 101st Airborne Brigade, a combat unit in the United States Army Vietnam or USARV pronounced USE-R-VEE. I am an advisor with Military Assistance Command Vietnam or MACV, pronounced MAC-VEE.

We shake hands, say good-bye; he turns and walks away. Looking at his receding back I sense relief—any obligation to him walks with him. My gut tells me he does not belong here.

Those going to MACV pick up our duffel bags and throw them in the back of a 2 1/2-ton truck. Then we load onto a blue painted school bus and ride into Saigon.

The Army forbids weapons in Saigon. Even our NCO guide is unarmed. The one indication that violence occurs is the thick wire mesh covering the open bus windows to stop grenades.

The bus drops us at the Koepler hotel, the processing center for MACV. Barbed wire and a brick wall surround the hotel. Armed Military Police in sandbag bunkers guard the entrance.

9

Our War

In Saigon MACV soldiers stay at hotels leased from the Vietnamese. The Vietnamese run them, billing the U.S. government. As the government not the guests pay, the Koepler's night clerk treats us with the same courtesy as if in a flophouse in New York's Bowery or San Francisco's Tenderloin.

After signing a register, the Vietnamese clerk tells me a room number on the fifth floor, handing me sheets and a blanket.

I enter the open-grill elevator like those Hollywood uses when creating a 1920's European scene—and ride it up.

On the fifth floor men sleep on cots crowded along the corridor's wall.

Surprisingly a bunk among the four double deck beds in my room is empty. I throw my duffel bag on it, undress, and go down the hall to shower in the common latrine. There is no hot water, the floor is flooded; the drain clogged. Three others from the flight are also attempting to shower. Giving up, I return to the room, toss my gear on the floor and fall asleep.

With first light my roommates are up, moving and talking. They have been here a couple of days and know where they are going. Now they wait for a flight upcountry or a vacancy in other less crowded MACV run hotels.

Going downstairs, I find the mess hall and have breakfast. The NCO guide from the night before tells me that everyone on last night's flight is to process in this morning; late in the afternoon we will hear a welcome speech from a General. Then we will wait for our field assignment.

We get our records processed, giving the pay and personnel file that we carried from our last duty station to a clerk.

Then briefed on the city.

"If you hear shooting and you're inside a building, get down under a bed or mattress—don't go to a window to see what it is—because the bomb that follows the shooting will blow glass slivers into you. Don't ride taxis that don't have handles on the inside of the door. Don't travel alone. Don't drink the water; it is not safe (all water

Getting There

comes from rooftop storage tanks in which herds of disease carrying rats live.) Don't get ice in your drinks, ice is made from water!"

On and on, the do and don'ts—then we are released. It is early, so I go for a walk.

The stench overwhelms. It is hot and steamy and though the Buddhist riots and garbage collectors strike are over, two story high garbage piles remain uncollected in the alleys.

Nuc-mam's odor, the Vietnamese diet's ever-present fish sauce, permeates the air.

You soon forget the heat and the smell, as you do the do and don'ts. If something happens it will, otherwise it won't.

The city bustles, the streets are crowded, the bus terminal swarms with Vietnamese. Goods fill the shops. The war is far away. I reach the Rex hotel—everyone goes to its roof bar—drink a beer and sit and talk—talk is expansive, everyone has a story. Then back to the Koepler. The General, his German accent makes him hard to understand, gives us a welcome speech—tomorrow we will have our orders.

Orders are posted on the bulletin board the next morning. I am going to the highlands as an infantry battalion advisor in II Corps—what I asked for.

Supply issues me a World War II M-2 carbine; the same obsolete weapon provided the Vietnamese soldiers I will work with. They also give me two empty ten round magazines. No bullets are issued. I will get ammo after going up country.

The Table of Allowances and Equipment authorizes me lightweight jungle fatigues, three sets, and jungle boots, two pairs. The canvas and leather jungle boots are made with drain holes on the side and removable metal insoles to stop punji stakes puncturing your foot.

The supply Sergeant has no jungle fatigues my size. He does find a pair of jungle boots although without the metal insoles, some well-worn load bearing equipment

Our War

(ammo pouches, backpack, canteen, first aid kit, and shoulder harness) along with a steel helmet and liner.

The next day I am off to the war, riding the blue bus back to Ton Son Nhut.

There I fill out a "shoe tag" with my name, rank and serial number, giving the bottom half to the boarding clerk in case the plane crashes, then board a C-119 flying upcountry to II Corps headquarters at Pleiku in Vietnam's mountainous central highlands.

But first we fly up the coast landing at Nah Trang, then Hue.

At Hue the C-119 has engine problems. The pilot tells us to off-load and wait on the bench along the wall inside a Quonset hut on the flight line while the engine is fixed.

Three American reporters burst into the hut; one with blood stains on his shirt. Finding a space on the bench, they sit laughing and joking with each other, bragging about their close calls. The Buddhists are rioting; they have their story and pictures, including Buddhists shot by the police. They give the film and hand written articles to the pilot to take back to Saigon.

The plane is ready; we fly onto Pleiku.

II Corps headquarters is housed in widely separated buildings that were once French Colonial offices. The surroundings are a pretty sea of tall green grass and shrubs. The weather is cool, a nice change from Saigon's heat and stench.

My orders are canceled. Corps gave the battalion advisor job to a Captain in the headquarters operations section. The personnel officer, the G-1, wants me to take his place.

I argue I want to see the war not stay in the rear. He offers me a ranger battalion if I agree to stay at Corps three months. Besides, "You'll probably get the battalion early, the Captain with them is the third one in the past five months." Ranger battalions are used as a relief force when someone screws up. They are routinely shot to

Getting There

pieces.

I do not hesitate saying "No."

He then tells me that the one other vacancy is as assistant district advisor in Darlac Province in the 23rd Division Tactical Zone.

This probably is the worst job he has but I do not want to stay at Corps; I agree to take it. He confirms my belief. I will replace a Captain evacuated because medics could not inoculate him against the bubonic plague rampant in the District.

The 23rd Division is in Ban Me Thuot, Darlac's capital. It is the next big city south on Highway 14, the main north-south road in the highlands. I have to wait for a flight, no military use the highway unless traveling in a convoy.

A small, one room, whitewashed building containing some GI cots is Pleiku's transient officer's quarters. An Australian Army Captain touring Vietnam on his annual leave along with Captain Campbell and I are staying there. Campbell is also waiting to fly to Ban Me Thuot.

In the evening, sipping warm beer, Campbell jokingly announces his plan to promote his career while avoiding getting shot. He will volunteer to be the Ban Me Thuot MACV headquarters commandant. To me it is a thankless job indulging officers outranking you, but he wants it. It will put him in the spotlight with access to senior officers.

Campbell shows us his leather briefcase with a large "Win in Vietnam" sticker on it. Laughing he says that when he gets to Ban Me Thuot and meets the senior Colonel, "I'll put the briefcase on my lap with the 'Win in Vietnam' sticker up so he can read it. He'll never send me to the field."

After two days, Campbell and I hitch a ride on the mail plane to Ban Me Thuot via Dalat.

The 23rd Division advisors Ban Me Thuot living quarters are in Bao Dai's

13

Our War

summer palace. The "playboy" prince, Bao Dai was the French installed puppet ruler before toppled by his Prime Minister, and Vietnam's subsequent President, Diem.

The palace is huge Montagnard long houses formed into an "H" held by thick wooden posts six feet off the ground. It is now the home for a few hundred 23rd Division and Darlac Province advisors.

Americans have added plumbing—flush toilets and hot and cold running water (fit to drink)—and proudly announce it on a large sign as you enter the compound courtyard. Sandbags, bunkers and barbed wire surround the compound adding a warlike ambiance to the buildings.

Most advisors spend their year tour here—playing volleyball, drinking cold beer at five cents a can, talking to other Americans, and listening to their Japanese stereos. Everything is purchased in the compound's PX at discounted prices.

All wait for their tour's end so they can return to the round doorknobs and round-eyes in the real world.

The American Colonel who advises the Vietnamese general commanding the 23rd Army Republic of Vietnam (ARVN pronounced R-Vin) Division runs the compound. He also commands all the American advisors working in the Provinces and Districts in the 23rd Division Tactical Zone.

The 23rd Division G-1 advisor, in his other role as the personnel officer for the 23rd Advisory Team, to which I am now assigned, confirms that I will be sent as the assistant advisor to a District north on Highway 14.

But first I am to make courtesy calls, in process again, and then wait on transportation going north; all of which will take several days.

The compound is full, but a battalion advisor is on an operation so I move into his vacant bunk. Campbell also finds a vacant space.

Next day, the two of us make a courtesy call on the Colonel now commanding us.

Campbell does as he said. He wears starched fatigues (the sleeves and trouser

14

Getting There

legs creased the night before with a steam iron he scrounged,) boots spit shined, hair cropped by a Vietnamese barber. He sits with the briefcase on his lap so that the Colonel sees the "Win in Vietnam" sign.

The Colonel, a shaved baldhead held in place by starched fatigues, talks about discipline (that is doing what he wants), and keeping physically fit (he is as thin as a rail.) Visibly impressed, the Colonel gives Campbell the headquarters job, then dismisses us.

Campbell smirks as we leave the Colonel's office; outside he laughs.

He is safe with maid service, hot and cold running water, and a soft bed every night besides booze, volleyball, and decent food. For a year he will do nothing but make work painting rocks or straightening and realigning sandbag seams or play military games such as guard or alert; total boredom.

To me only the war is interesting; I want to see it. Besides it is not in me to cater to superiors.

In processing again, I fill out address change cards to forward my mail and pay. I give my clothing records to the supply Sergeant to order my missing jungle fatigues and boots.

Then I meet my new boss—a Major, the district advisor.

He is in Ban Me Thuot recovering from pleurisy and bunking in a room off the verandah that runs around the long house.

I knock at his door and introduce myself. Stepping outside onto the deck, he walks to the outside railing, telling me he does not want anyone in the room to overhear.

Dressed in fatigue trousers, a white T-shirt, with flip-flops on his feet, he grabs the railing with both hands. Looking into the distance, he starts talking in a monologue, initially in a soft, low southern drawl, then anger takes over, his white skin glistens with sweat.

He is mad: mad at the Vietnamese, mad at the United States Army and mad at the Province advisory staff for whom we work.

15

Our War

Short, balding, with light skin that readily burns to a bright red in the sun, his squat build slowly turning from muscle to fat, in his mid thirties but looking older, he looks what he is, a southern red neck.

"The District you've been assigned to," he tells me, "is a hell hole. The Army sends us out there but gives us no support. I'm here recovering from pleurisy because of the bad living conditions. We're supposed to have a building to live in, but there's none. We've been living in a bunker—that's what made me sick. I can't get Province to do anything for us; all they care about is staying safe here in Ban Me Thuot. They won't raise a finger to help us; you can't even count on them getting mail or supplies to us.

Everything in the District is primitive; we are the first Americans there. We moved into it in March. The Captain you're replacing left because he can't be vaccinated for the bubonic plague, which is epidemic there. Everybody on the team would like to leave; I can't believe the Army allows us to live like this.

You know I've been in the Army since the War. When I was sixteen I enlisted; my father was a farmer, a mean drunk; I'd do anything to get out of there. That's the reason I don't drink; I'm a Baptist.

During the war I was at the tail end driving a tank into Germany. The Army took care of you then. I decided to stay in and made Sergeant in the infantry. My unit was sent from Japan when the North Koreans crossed the 38th. At Pusan I got a battlefield commission. Pusan was bad. The North Koreans would attack pushing women and children in front. We shot them all." As he talks my mind wanders to Simon De Montfort telling the Crusaders to distinguish the Catholics from the Albigenses by killing them all and "Let God decide."

He continues to rant on. "I fought all the way to the Yalu and back. All that time though nothing was as Godforsaken as the way the Army treats us now. We can't get supplies, the living conditions are awful, and Province won't help.

You know, under Army regulations, it was mandatory I retire last year. I bought a fifty thousand dollar grader on credit to go into business for myself; now it's

Getting There

sitting idle and I'm losing money." As he says this he hits the railing with his fist.

"They can't even get my wife's letters to me to tell me how the business is doing. The Army involuntarily extends me and sends me to this hellhole; can you explain to me why we are here? The Vietnamese are worthless, corrupt and lazy, they won't fight."

Now, continuously hitting his open left hand palm with his right rolled into a fist, his face glistening with sweat, he continues, "It's hard to talk to them; we don't even have a regular interpreter. Some Vietnamese are OK but a lot are cowards. They don't want to fight.

At District, we do everything for ourselves. I get along with Na Han the District chief, he's Montagnard. The Montagnards aren't too bad. Before I left, I got him to give me part of a building to use as a sleeping area. I also traded with Special Forces and got Claymores and BAR's. That is the way we've been able to survive—doing it ourselves. You'll see tomorrow. We'll fly up there in the morning. Meet me outside the main gate at ten and we'll drive to the airfield."

Saying this he hits the railing with both hands turns and walks into his room.

That the Major dislikes the Vietnamese is no surprise. No American in country seems to like them.

A popular joke among the GI's is "Do you know how to win in Vietnam?"

"Load all the Vietnamese on our side on boats and sail them into the Pacific—then nuke the country."

(A short pause) "Then sink the boats!"

The Major, as do most Americans, likes the Montagnards. Like the Americans the "Yards" loathe the Vietnamese.

The "Yards" are split into different aboriginal tribes living in isolated hamlets, normally called Buon or Ban something or other, in the mountainous backbone that runs Vietnam's length until it flattens out in the Mekong delta.

Our War

Most Montagnards in Darlac Province are Rhade. Taller and darker skinned than the Vietnamese, they depict themselves to those Americans who listen as suffering the same fate as the American Indian.

The Vietnamese play the white settler's role. Moving from the north they had conquered the southern coastal plain before the French arrived in the 19th century.

However, the French stopped the Vietnamese moving into the highlands. It was not done from altruism but to keep the highlands for large French tea and coffee plantations. The Montagnards, nevertheless, view the French as their protectors—and now look for the same from the Americans. Many Montagnards served in the French army against the Viet Minh.

After the French withdrawal, Diem settled North Vietnamese Catholic refugees in the highlands. They were given large undeveloped land tracts.

Diem also forcibly resettled rebellious peasants from the coastal plain.

While the Catholics are staunch government supporters, the rebels aid the Viet Cong (VC) and now the invading North Vietnamese Army (NVA) as it comes south. Diem seeded the base so helpful to the North Vietnamese while angering the "Yards."

To resist Vietnamese settlement the Montagnards started their own independence movement, *"Front Unifie Pour La Liberation Des Races Opprimees"* or *"FULRO."* One job for the CIA and American Special Forces is to try to control *"FULRO."*

The next morning a jeep carries the Major and me out along Highway 14. The airstrip, guarded by lethargic Vietnamese Regional Force soldiers living in large sandbag bunkers, is located on the town's outskirts before the highway begins heading due north through the French owned plantations.

An American assault helicopter company makes the airfield its home. We are not flying with them, however, but rather with Darlac Province aviation support, pilots and door gunners in a helicopter from Pleiku.

Getting There

Our flights destination is Buon Ho, the largest District in land area but least populated with a little over thirty thousand, mostly Montagnards, in it

The Major and I crawl into the chopper and find a place to sit among the food crates and 55-gallon gas drums.

The motor revs, the crew chief climbs in. The chopper wobbles and we lift off. We fly north at 1000 feet following Highway 14 for about 25 miles.

The day is clear. Except for the thick green plantations right after take off, the land below is flat, deserted and desolate. Interspersed are small, red dust covered hamlets, tiny thatched roof houses tucked along the road's edge

Fifteen minutes out the chopper rises over a large hill; on the backside a green valley stretches out before us. A large hamlet sits at the hill's bottom.

In the distance, on the highway's left sits a small pimple; its slopes are barren, the top covered with barbed wire, bunkers, trench line, and several buildings grouped together.

Hamlets cluster around the hill's base as if it shelters them from the surrounding evil.

Green smoke rises near the pimple's top on the clear ground immediately outside the perimeter wire. The chopper hovers over the smoke then drops to the ground.

An American Army Sergeant quickly drives up in a jeep pulling a trailer. The chopper's blades continue to rotate. We talk by shouting into each other's ear. The supplies are hurriedly thrown into the trailer.

The empty helicopter lifts from the ground and heads back south to Ban Me Thuot.

I climb into the jeep's back seat while the Major gets in next to the driver.

We head into the compound, my home for the next year.

Our War

The road into Buon Ho District Headquarters.

Buon Ho

CHAPTER TWO

The compound is about 100 yards square.

Over three hundred people live and work in the compound. Besides an ARVN howitzer section, Regional Force company, District staff, police and Americans, there are five platoons of Popular Force soldiers, along with wives and children, as well as a half-track and crew.

Driving in we pass barbed wire fences with interlaced trip wires—then a ditch, the sides and bottom covered with punji stakes—before coming to the parapet, an earthen mound three feet high with a trench behind, parts with overhead cover. Wood bunkers are on the corners.

Only where the road comes through the entrance gate is the compound's perimeter without ditch, fighting trench and permanent barbed wire barrier.

Here, portable barbed wire barriers tangled together, are pulled open in the morning and pushed closed at dusk. This is our one daytime guard post.

A large bunker, used when needed as the local jail, faces the compound entrance.

The District chief's office is directly behind this bunker in a long single story building built with stucco-covered cinder blocks painted white.

That paint job is now a dingy red. The ground in the compound is red clay. The top layer, pounded down by the continual daily traffic in and out, is a fine dry red dust. Whipped by the wind, it coats the building.

A wide verandah runs along the building's front. At its south end are the District's military offices-operations and intelligence.

At the north end is a small room that the advisors use both as office and kitchen. Jammed in there are our propane fed stove and refrigerator as well as a dining table, chairs, two desks and a filing cabinet.

Na Han, the District chief, has his office in a large room entered through two doors in the building's center. His beat up mahogany desk is near the room's back wall, directly across but some distance from the doors. A large 1 to 25,000-scale Province map hangs on a sidewall.

Everyone talking to him stands. His desk and chair are the only furniture.

His sleeping quarters are two tiny rooms behind the office.

Southwest behind Na Han's office is a rambling single story wooden building. It is the sleeping quarters for the compound's two-gun 105-MM ARVN howitzer section as well as the Regional Force company commander and his officers.

The howitzers with their fire direction center are located in the rear. Firing 360 degrees up to 11.5 kilometers, their range fan establishes the limits of District control–11.5 kilometers in any direction. At night the guns fire harassment and interdiction out to the fan's limit. You learn to sleep through it.

Government supporters live within the artillery fan, the reason the hamlets are clustered around the District headquarters. Outside the fan belongs to whosoever is in that space with the most force.

The District administration building with its civilian clerks and District administrator is located in a one story wooden building on the compound's north side. Here births and deaths are registered, land transactions recorded, identity cards issued, and government petitions filed. The Popular Force muster rolls and supply records are also here. Half the building is a large room used for District meetings.

Na Han's chief civilian administrator is a distinguished looking, gray hair, French educated, elderly Rhade. The remaining staff is both Montagnard and Vietnamese.

The police station, directly to the administration building's east, is a small one-room building where the District's police chief has his office.

Further north behind these two buildings is the "Co-loc-bo" or troop canteen now used as the sleeping quarters for the Americans and some Vietnamese Sergeants on the District staff.

All buildings have dirt floors except the cement one in the District chief's office.

The Vietnamese government copied the centralized French political system. The civilian government in Saigon dictates everything through the Provinces (equivalent to an American state) and Districts (similar to an American county), to the villages and hamlets.

The smallest political unit is the hamlet, thatched huts or Montagnard long houses clustered together; a village is normally several scattered hamlets. In the central highlands there are also cantons, which contain two or three villages.

Superimposed on this civilian administration is a military government. Every orientation on Vietnam starts with the rote phase, "Vietnam is divided into four Corps," a lead line with a good ring to it since Caesar wrote his *Commentaries*.

Corps assigns Provinces to each ARVN division. The ARVN division commander, like a Chinese warlord, is boss. His ARVN regulars have the combat power.

The Corps commander also assigns a military commander to each Province—called a Sector in military parlance—and to the District—called a sub-Sector.

The military commander is dual hatted; he is also the civilian government's Province or District chief.

My job is to be the number two on a six man American advisor team to Na Han, the District chief, in his military role as sub–Sector chief.

Province and District chiefs have their own soldiers, Regional and Popular Force, called "Ruff-Puffs" by their American advisors.

The Regional Force (RF) soldiers are full time but cannot be transferred outside the Province.

Our Regional Force company has two obsolete thirty-caliber machine guns, and

Our War

two 60-MM mortars. The company is so undermanned, about 50 men, that in the field we take one each. Most soldiers are armed with, to the small Vietnamese, a heavy World War II semiautomatic, eight shot M-1 rifle; others carry Thompson submachine guns or lighter M-1 or M-2 carbines with either ten or twenty round clips. To improve the odds against the carbine's tendency to jam, clips are never fully loaded helping the magazine spring retain its compression.

The Regional Force enlisted are mostly Rhade Montagnards. The officers are Vietnamese from Saigon, drafted for the duration. The one exception is Warrant Officer Duc. Educated in France, he is the Montagnard token officer assigned the company.

Most Rhade speak French and some Vietnamese as well as Rhade. Nearly all served with the French. Some Regional Force soldiers like Duc served with Special Forces in the Civilian Irregular Defense Group (CIDG) and speak passable English. French, however, remains the *lingua franca* for Vietnamese has many dialects while the northern dialect is often incomprehensible to the southerner. Communications are enhanced by suitable gestures.

The Popular Force (PF) are a hamlet's part time soldiers, issued antique shotguns and 1903 Springfields, often in disrepair, and asked to defend their hamlet. They get a small monthly stipend in rice and money.

The Popular Force platoons in the compound are Rhade, ex-French colonial soldiers whose hamlets are outside the artillery fan. Older men, in their late 30's to middle 50's, they have withdrawn to the safety of the District headquarters.

Our major concern if attacked is a small ridge that runs north 400 meters from the compound's perimeter to a tree-covered hill higher in elevation. The brush has been cleared from the ridge to provide fields of fire. The elevated hill is the problem. Crew served weapons placed there can fire directly down into the compound. The same mentality that picked the site for Dien Bien Phu chose this one.

Buon Ho

Our Popular Force man the trench facing the ridge. Dirt dug from the trench is piled in front then reinforced by timber as an escarpment. Firing ports are cut into the escarpment. Thick logs covered with dirt run overhead from the escarpment to a few feet behind the trench.

A thatch roof runs two feet above the overhead cover. Dual purposed it keeps rain out while also acting as a standoff. The hope is that incoming shells have contact fuses that explode hitting the standoff rather than delay fuses that blast through the overhead cover.

The PF's family lives with him in the trenches. The family area is the small space between the trench and where the overhead logs touch the ground. Here are their sleeping mats, cooking fires and small personal items.

Conditions in the compound are harsh but the Montagnard PF still has his long house in some outlying Buon. The families split their time between visiting their father or husband and staying at the Buon. The men furtively visit them when they feel there is little chance of anything happening.

The field uniform for the Regional and Popular Force as well as ARVN is olive green fatigues. This helps distinguish them from the Viet Cong who generally wear traditional Vietnamese black pajamas, or the North Vietnamese in khaki.

Other armed men are also found in a District. Among them are Hamlet Youth– people believed friendly to the government and given weapons—or members of CIA sponsored organizations: Truong Son, Provincial Reconnaissance Units (later the basis for the Phoenix program), and Hamlet Redevelopment teams. Border Provinces have CIDG. Many people live off the war.

FULRO is strong in the District particularly among those Rhade who served in the CIDG.

The CIDG rebelled last year at Buon Brieng in the District's north. They shot

Our War

their Vietnamese officers. The American Special Forces advisor managed to stop the massacre, but the camp was abandoned.

Na Han, a Jerai Montagnard who looks like a dark version of the French movie actor Yves Montand, was appointed chief to appease the District's Montagnards.

His appointment is in keeping with Saigon's belief that you govern best by diluting local authority. Most Jerai live in Pleiku Province to the north. His tribal differences with the Rhade produces almost the same hostility as if he was Vietnamese.

The Vietnamese officers on his staff further weaken his authority. Military decisions need the Province chief's approval, and also Lieutenant Thieu's, the District's intelligence officer. Thieu, from Saigon, in his late twenties, is slightly built with wispy chin hairs and a pinkie fingernail several inches long. In the Chinese mandarin tradition it indicates a scholar above doing manual work. He looks like a Fu Manchu caricature.

Thieu does not hide his disdain for the Americans, who lack his combat experience, or the Montagnards, who are his racial inferiors. His office next to Na Han's ensures he sees everyone Na Han meets.

Na Han makes no effort to hide his misery as District chief. As a Jerai he has no social life with either the Rhade or Vietnamese. In the evening he retires to the back room behind his office with his two Jerai bodyguards for company. His wife and children live in Cheo Reo.

One evening his loneliness drives him into our office. Over a few beers he talks candidly. He speaks both French and English. "The District is not good for my family. I know no one here. Jerai are better than Rhade. Rhade nam-pay is no good; when the Jerai make nam-pay, we add blood to it. That's the way to make good nam-pay." Saying this he rolls his tongue around his mouth as he recalls the delicious taste of Jerai nam-pay, the Montagnard's home brew.

"Living here with the Rhade," he continues, "is making me sick to my stomach. Cheo Reo is much better. I am building a big house there for my family. As soon as I can I want to go back to the army, I'm not making enough money here to put up with the problems." His goal is to get out from the District with some money without incurring his commander's wrath. This includes keeping the American District advisors happy by catering to our physical needs

Our advisor team, besides the Major and myself, are two Sergeants, Bearfoot for operations, Dian for training, along with Specialist Powers our medic and Private Stedman our radio operator. Though the team members, like all soldiers, talk little about their life in the "world," living together reveals enough for each to form an opinion on the others

Stedman, from outside Detroit, drafted right after high school, is all American, a natural soldier; six foot tall, strong, intelligent and enthusiastic. A Private First Class serving his two years, the war is an interesting experience, something to talk about at American Legion meetings after he gets out and goes home. His future is already decided: a girl back home and a well paying job as a union carpenter and contractor.

Powers, a Specialist Five, raised by his mother, is from a small town in Pennsylvania. He enlisted and is now heading towards his four-year enlistment's end.

His ambition is to be a doctor— he subscribes to medical book clubs and journals and constantly reads them. He even looks like a doctor, wearing thick black horn rimmed glasses, a white smock over his fatigues, a stethoscope hanging from his neck as he treats his daily patient load at the District hospital. Running the District hospital, he is as close as he will ever come to being a real doctor, for now he is "Doc" to everyone in the District. He talks about leaving the Army but all know he has found his home.

The two NCOs are contrasts.

Dian, the training Sergeant, is a thin, muscular, agitated, airborne infantry soldier. Barracks educated, he constantly reads books on history, politics and philosophy. Opinionated, he loves to argue on any subject. Married and divorced, the Army is his life and love.

He tells you that the war gives meaning to his existence. He is in the Army not for the three squares and a flop, but because combat, its violence and danger, excites him. While he enjoys good food or a soft bed, real gratification comes from the kill after sitting for hours in an ambush, or walking miles to raid a village or directing gunships onto a target. He wants to leave the District and get into an American combat unit.

Bearfoot, the operations Sergeant, with over twenty years of service, is a military careerist. A good "ole" southern country boy, his concern is the here and now. This Army like all armies provides that by giving him the good life: booze, women, and as little work as possible. In exchange he periodically puts his life on the line. All he wants is to survive as comfortably as he can.

Though supposedly the operations Sergeant, Bearfoot's real job is unit cook and all around handyman. Working all day over a stove he does not have to deal with the Vietnamese or leave the compound's safety. Obtaining food and other supplies guarantees a weekly overnight trip to Ban Me Thuot and his Vietnamese shack job.

Bearfoot and the Major are best buddies.

Buon Ho

The barbed wire fences and trench

Captain Na Han, District chief.

Buon Ho

LT. Thieu, District Intelligence officer

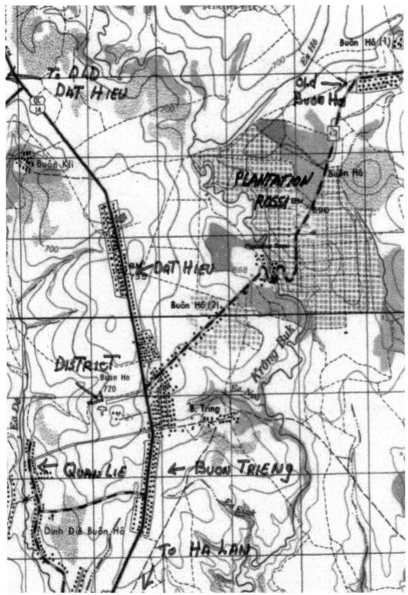

Army Map Service, Buon Ho District, (1973 Map)

On Our Own

CHAPTER THREE

The team's AM radios are our lifeline to the outside world. Only the AM radios reach Ban Me Thuot. A bunker contains both our AM Motorola commercial single side band, as well as a military AN GRC-9.

The Motorola is voice operated. The AN GRC-9, operated with a Teletype key, requires an operator who can transmit and receive Morse code. Only Stedman knows Morse code.

Our FM radio for local communications is also there.

The team's ammunition, medical supplies, large rattraps and cans of D-Con are stored in the bunker.

At night large rats roam the bunkers. That is no surprise considering the people crammed into the compound.

In the evening traps are put out and D-Con spread. The operator, if manning the radio at night, keeps a baseball bat handy to hit the more aggressive. Heavy mosquito netting pulled down while sleeping to protect from mosquitoes also offers an obstacle to the rats. In the morning dead rats are outside the bunker or where they dragged themselves after the traps break their backs.

This is our fighting position if attacked.

Stedman and Powers sleep in the radio bunker.

Bearfoot sleeps by himself in another nearby bunker.

The Major and Dian sleep in the "Co-loc-bo"; I decide to sleep there.

The "Co-loc-bo" is a large wooden frame building covered with a sheet metal roof and sidings. The floor is dirt. At one end a bamboo wall separates the advisor sleeping area from that used by the Vietnamese Sergeants.

Next to the "Co-loc-bo" is our latrine. Each morning PF carry water buckets up the compound hill from a creek five hundred meters away to fill our 55-gallon drum mounted on a wooden scaffold 12 feet above the ground next to the latrine. A pipe

33

extends from the drum's bottom to a spigot used either to shower or to run water into a basin for shaving and washing. A brick wall encloses the shower. Next to it, also enclosed, is the French style toilet—a hole in the ground that you straddle.

The compound's Vietnamese do not have these luxuries. They walk to the stream to wash (except for the officers who have water carried to them.) Their latrine is a hole in the ground out in the perimeter wire. A bamboo screen facing the compound provides privacy.

The first evening, Bearfoot, after slaving all day over the hot stove, serves a great meal. Army number 10 can vegetables (vegetables from an Army Standard Issued Ration can that feeds ten men) with roast beef and hot biscuits washed down with Bier La Rue.

Bier La Rue is best described as tasting like formaldehyde. Not my favorite but the Ban Me Thuot PX cannot stock enough American beer to meet demand.

With the PX constantly out, the team contracts to have Bier La Rue brought each week from Ban Me Thuot by a Lambretta driver, the civilian attired ARVN Lieutenant who runs the local spy nets. Each week he supplements his income by delivering us fifty bottles in a burlap sack. It also provides an excuse for him to come into the District compound.

After supper we sit, talk, and play Hearts, drink tea or beer, until one by one we go to our bunks. The local French plantation supplies the tea. Unlike the insipid warm water that Americans call tea, this is a dark and bitter liquid made from ground leaves drunk without cream or sugar. Our bodies grow to demand it. Pots of it are consumed each evening and for breakfast.

The next morning, after breakfast, the Major takes me touring the District. Once we leave the compound, we travel armed—though relatively safe as long as we stay in the populated area, no more then four or five miles from the District headquarters.

We tour the hamlets: Dat Hieu, Ha Lan, Buon Trieng, and Quan Lie, each with

On Our Own

log palisades, bunkers, and thatched and wooden huts with dirt floors. The farmers are planting rice in the fields, while the hamlets are filled with people moving along the dusty streets, seemingly busy—you wonder where they are going in these empty lands.

At the base of the compound hill, where hardtop Highway 14 intersects the dirt road running east to old Buon Ho, is the original District's ruins, a partially damaged cement building that was the District headquarters, three destroyed cement bunkers, and some still used wooden buildings.

The surrounding area is overgrown with thick brush except for well-worn paths.

"Stay away from the brush," the Major says. "Mines are buried there."

Small shops line the dirt road running easterly to old Buon Ho.

Near the ruined District headquarters is the local garage; a metal covered wood shack with a thatched hut behind.

Our two Japanese built Kaiser jeeps are junk, rough riding and uncomfortable. Their advantage is that the garage can repair them.

Next to the garage is a two-chair barbershop. Nearby are stores in unpainted, weathered, wooden buildings selling metal trunks made from pressed beer cans, cloth, t-shirts, thread, beads and needles, cooking oil, nuc-mam tins, sacks of rice, pots, pans and cheap ceramic china plates and cups. There is even a coffee shop/bar in a thatch hut with a few worn tables and chairs outdoors.

The Major says one shop belongs to the leading merchant, Madame Ba, the former District chief's widow; he was killed when the Viet Cong overran the old District headquarters.

Periodically she drives her jeep into the compound to tell Na Han how to better run the District. A slightly overweight imperious figure in her mid-forties, her redeeming feature is three attractive daughters that help in her store.

35

Our War

The hamlet ends where the dirt road curves down to a ford and the river.

A two story concrete mansion sits atop a small bluff to the left on the curve. Rossi Plantation, a French owned coffee and tea plantation stretches from here for several kilometers along the dirt road.

The Major drives up to the mansion. Stephanau, the French man running the plantation is not there. His Vietnamese foreman tells us he has gone to Ban Me Thuot.

The Major then drives to the ford.

Three Montagnard women with their young children are washing clothes. The women are clad in the traditional long, wrap around, Montagnard black skirt hanging from the waist to slightly above their bare feet. When visiting a hamlet they may wear a blouse or a more traditional black shawl over the upper part of their body. Today they are bare breasted.

I feel like a voyeur looking at the naked aboriginal women featured monthly in the *National Geographic*. But there is no erotic thought. They are grossly unattractive with sagging breasts and red betel nut stained teeth, seen as they smile and wave at us.

Driving back to the compound on Highway 14, the Major points out several wooden buildings at the compound's hill's base. Two are long, low barracks, which the District's Sergeants share, several families to a room.

There is also a larger building, completely open in the front, with trucks and Lambrettas parked around it. People are sitting on benches at long wooden tables placed on the packed dirt floor.

This is "Howard Johnson's" the Major explains, the local restaurant. Its claim to fame is a propane fed refrigerator enabling it to serve cold beer and soda, while milk for "cafe-au-lait" and beef for "bifteck" is unspoiled. In the morning it sells fresh French bread brought daily by Lambretta from Ban Me Thuot. Vietnamese on the District staff eat here.

Pointing to a small wooden building next to the restaurant, the Major tells me

On Our Own

that I can get my fatigues washed and pressed there. The building is the District public affairs office. An ARVN officer's widow runs it and makes extra money washing and ironing fatigues. While not thinking about it at the time, in the months to come often the one female contact for a week would be small talk with the widow delivering or picking up laundry.

Returning to the compound, the rest of the day passes in talking—there is little to do.

The Vietnamese run the District, we are advisors. We do not direct or control, we give advice; we are consultants. It is up to the Vietnamese to do or not to do.

We have little interaction with the Vietnamese. Na Han and some officers speak a little English—but no advisor speaks Vietnamese and our interpreter Nguyen is AWOL.

Nguyen shows up a few days later.

From Saigon, Nguyen ran a thriving business guiding foreign big game hunters during Diem's Presidency. The fighting and Diem's murder killed that business.

Though on the outs with the current regime, he is working on a deal to transport vegetables from Dalat to Saigon. But government bureaucrats are holding up the shipments, spoiling them. He needs to get back to Saigon to make the connections and pay the bribes to get his shipments through. This war is not his problem.

When Nguyen tells us he is going to Ban Me Thuot, it is anyone's guess if or when he will return. The Vietnamese at Province provide the interpreters and control their availability. When we complain after Nguyen is gone for a week or so, Province sends Dong. Dong is around a week or two, then he is gone. Sometime later, after again complaining, Nguyen shows up for a short period before again disappearing. Dong returns but eventually he too disappears. We operate without an interpreter.

Little is done.

That is fine with the Major and Bearfoot. They are concerned with their living conditions, not the war.

Our War

Americans take their luxurious life, hot meals, refrigerated foods, running water with hot baths and flush toilets, entertainment (radio, TV or movies), heated and air-conditioned buildings, for granted. While such good living is not expected in combat, we are not in combat; we are advisors. United States Army Regulations authorize this good life for advisors. But as the Major told me there is a difference between what is authorized and what we get.

We devote our time improving our life style and dealing with requirements generated from MACV.

I read the *Army Handbook for District Advisors*, the Army "bible" on how we are to operate. I set up accounts to obtain free books and a movie projector from Special Services.

Because we are an "isolated" unit, I request that the team get issued 10 man packs. Surprisingly, the chain of command agrees and every few weeks a box containing free tobacco, candies, soap, shaving gear, books and writing materials arrives.

The Major submits the paperwork for the prefabricated building and the two 100 kilowatt generators authorized. All fantasize over the prefab building design in the *Handbook* with its indoor plumbing, ceiling fans and kitchen.

Fifty-pounds of steaks that Bearfoot scrounges from the Ban Me Thuot mess Sergeant are traded for a Special Forces excess 10 KW generator. The generator provides electricity for the radios, light bulbs in our office and as a goodwill gesture, lights in Na Han's sleeping area.

The team already has the propane cooking stove, refrigerator and rattan furniture (stuffed couch and two chairs) authorized.

The biggest improvement is getting hot water.

An immersion heater (designed to heat water in a field kitchen) is bartered from the MACV mess hall in Ban Me Thuot and hooked up to the fifty-five gallon drum containing our wash water. Now we get hot water for showers or shaving by climbing the

On Our Own

ladder to the latrine roof, lighting the heater on the drum, and then waiting fifteen minutes for the water to heat.

Stedman, a product of middle class America where cleanliness is next to godliness, loves the hot water. He starts taking two or three showers a day. Within a few days his entire body breaks out in a black bumpy skin rash. The Army doctors in Ban Me Thuot are mystified but suggest he take fewer showers. He does; the rash goes away.

The PF are happy too; they are hauling a lot less water.

A few days after I arrive, Sergeant Y'Duc, the Montagnard intelligence Sergeant who works for Lieutenant Thieu, comes into our office. He speaks some English having served with the American Special Forces at Dak To.

With him is an old, dark skin Montagnard about 5 feet tall, carrying a small ax, dressed in loincloth and dark pullover shirt. Fat, ugly, and dirty, the old man is so grimy it is difficult to tell where his skin ends and clothes begin.

Y'Duc says the man has information that he wants me to hear.

The little man spits his information out, speaking first in Rhade with Y'Duc translating, then switching to a bastardized French when he realizes I speak a little.

Excitedly he tells me there are "Beaucoup VC." The Viet Cong are going to the hamlets collecting rice and directing ladder building, telling the people that a large North Vietnamese Army unit is coming to attack the District. (The ladders will be thrown over the compound's barbed wire in an attack. Afterwards they will use them to carry away the dead and wounded.)

I have 20,000 P's in a revolving slush fund from the Province intelligence advisor to pay for intelligence. The money is not audited; my only requirement is a signature. Y'Duc knows about the fund and brought in the old "Yard" for me to pay him. I give the old man a few hundred P's. He smiles and leaves.

Although the official exchange rate is about a hundred P's to the dollar, a few hundred P's is a lot in this poor land. A Popular Force soldier's monthly salary is 300 P's.

Our War

Y'Duc says the old man is a former French soldier now on the District payroll as the hamlet chief for a hamlet outside the artillery fan; "He is a good man and always speaks the truth."

Y'Duc signs the voucher that the money was paid for intelligence information.

Next day, an L-19 "Bird-dog" buzzes the compound, flying low over the "Co-loc-bo's" roof. This signals that the pilot wants us to come up on the radio and talk to him.

Stedman turns on the FM radio.

The pilot tells us to clear Highway 14 so he can land.

The Major cleared a dirt runway using a borrowed bulldozer from the Rossi plantation. But the strip has not been checked out and approved by an instructor pilot. Until then the highway is our landing strip.

Na Han, the Major and the rest get into the jeeps and rush down the hill to the highway.

Traffic is stopped; the plane lands. A crowd quickly gathers. The L-19, a single engine slow flying plane, has two seats. The pilot sits in the front with the passenger in the rear seat.

Lieutenant Colonel Ireland, the Province advisor, climbs out from the rear seat.

Shaking hands, he stands next to the plane on the highway. "Information has been received," he says, "that a large North Vietnamese Army unit is moving into this District. Word is that their objective is to overrun a District headquarters, probably yours. The 23rd Division commander thinks this is disinformation; the NVA objective is Ban Me Thuot and any attack on you will be a diversion.

I came to tell you that if attacked no relief force will come.

You are on your own."

Then handing us our mail and pulling out a case of Budweiser propped behind the back seat he climbs into the seat and the plane takes off.

On Our Own

Knowing we are abandoned rouses the Major. We drive up the hill to the compound and walk into Na Han's office to talk about preparing the compound for an attack. We need to drill the garrison on what to do if attacked, have a practice alert and test fire the weapons—in addition, the perimeter barriers need repair and the bunkers rebuilt and reinforced.

To our surprise Na Han says no. He insists no one is going to attack. The Major argues but Na Han wont budge.

Finally Na Han reveals "I have an uncle with the VC; if there is an attack he will tell me."

Neither the Major nor I share his faith in his uncle. Finally, to calm us down, he agrees to test fire the weapons.

At dusk, after locking the gate, we test fire the weapons. All the crew served and automatic weapons, the thirty-caliber machine-gun, Browning automatic rifles (BAR's) and the fifty-caliber machine-gun mounted in the half-track are fired. There is a tremendous racket with tracers bouncing off the ground to our front making bright fireworks.

The Regional Force company's thirty-caliber machine-gun mounted on the southwest corner bunker fires a few rounds. Then it jams. Dian adjusts the headspace and gets it firing, now joined by the BAR's.

The Major in trading with Special Forces obtained, besides the generator, twenty BAR's (automatic weapons with twenty round magazines) as well as trip flares, Claymores and a fifty-five gallon drum of defoliant. The BAR's, trip flares and Claymores were given to the Montagnards and placed on the compound's side facing the ridge running north. All twenty BAR's are now firing.

Suddenly one of the tracers from the fifty-caliber hits a trip flare in the barbed wire. The perimeter lights up. The dry grass in the wire bursts into flame.

Na Han orders everyone to stop firing. He yells at two Popular Force soldiers to

Our War

go into the wire and stamp out the fire.

Passing through a hole in the barbed wire fence, they reach the flames and jump up and down trying to stomp it out. It still spreads.

With the fire spreading, Na Han yells at them to move away. As they walk away a Claymore explodes blowing the fire out.

This ends the test firing. We go back to our office and drink the Budweiser.

Next morning the soldiers on the half-track are packing their gear.

Na Han, standing nearby, tells me Province ordered the half-track back to Ban Me Thuot. Last night the one at the Mewal plantation outpost was destroyed and the crew killed by Viet Cong using a B-40, a Russian version of the World War II German antitank Panzerfaust.

Province is going to keep this half-track locked up in Ban Me Thuot so it is not lost.

The following morning, two Popular Force walk into the compound with a khaki uniformed soldier. One PF carries both an AK-47 assault rifle and his M-1.

The khaki clad man claims he voluntarily surrendered as a "Chieu-Hoi."

The "Chieu-Hoi" says he is a North Vietnamese Lieutenant. His feet swelled up on the long walk down from the north on the "Ho Chi Minh" trail. He used this as an excuse to fall behind his Regiment, 18B. Once separated he headed to Highway 14 and gave up to the first South Vietnamese he found, the Popular Force guarding the gate to Dat Hieu.

A Hanoi College graduate, like his American college contemporaries, he does not want to participate in this war.

Within two hours he is gone by helicopter to Ban Me Thuot. District receives no feedback; the NVA Lieutenant and whatever information he has disappears into the intelligence void at Ban Me Thuot.

On Our Own

That night an encoded message comes over our single side band ordering Na Han to open the Ha Lan pass on Highway 14 in the morning.

A convoy will be coming north from Ban Me Thuot.

The Popular Force platoons at Ha Lan are given the job. This village, settled by Catholics who fled the north, sits at the foot of the pass between the District and Ban Me Thuot.

The pass is dangerous, a narrow road cut into the hillside. At the top a bluff with a flat overlook rises on one side about thirty feet above the road. The other side is a steep drop off. Blocking the road's crest with a barricade will stop a vehicle. Then anyone lying in wait on the bluff's top can fire down killing the occupants.

The convoy arrives in the morning. It is moving supplies.

Special Forces is opening Buon Bleck camp in the north near abandoned Buon Brieng. Rumors about the camp exist but this is the first official word that it is actually going in.

The camp commander, a newly promoted Special Forces Captain, has come south to meet the convoy.

Special Forces original concept was to operate as small teams training guerrilla bands in Eastern Europe behind Russian lines. Many original members were displaced persons with World War II military experience who found a home in the American Army.

Now Special Forces is expanding hurriedly to meet the war's combat wastage. The Captain is the new breed; in the Army a couple of years, he exudes arrogance, believing it compensates for his inexperience. The Major asks the Captain if he is interested in joint operations with the District; the Captain responds he is too busy.

An ARVN infantry battalion riding in 2 1/2-ton trucks protects the convoy.

The battalion advisor and I served in the same brigade in Germany.

Our relationship was not the best.

He and his wife lived in the same military housing apartment building as my

Our War

wife and I. They had no children; she worked. Rumor had it that she had been an airline stewardess. Though a little plump she was attractive and conveyed the impression that she was entitled.

Around seven one morning, I came out to go to work. Her Volkswagen was next to mine. She was trying to get it started and was agitated when it would not. Leaving her car, she ran over to me as I started to back out, asking me to help her. She was going to be late and her husband was on an exercise in Turkey. I told her I had to go but she could get someone from the PX garage, about a block away to help. I then drove off.

I gave her no more thought. Other things were on my mind. I was running late that morning for my nuclear weapon storage site inspection by the Inspector General from Headquarters, U.S. Army Europe. In the peacetime Army failing this type inspection could be disastrous to a military career. At least one classmate thought so, committing suicide after failing one in Korea.

Her husband burst into my office a week after his return from Turkey. He was fuming, spitting out his words, angrily telling me that his wife was late to work because she had to ask a "Negro" officer (she was from the south) in another stairwell to push her car to the PX garage.

The husband had been pussy whipped. I answered simply "Better her late than me." An act speaks for itself.

After that they did not talk to me.

Today, on Highway 14, we are best buddies.

The convoy moves on through the District heading north. The next day it passes rapidly heading south.

The battalion advisor maintains radio contact with division through our FM station. The Vietnamese radios, World War II models, are out of range of Ban Me Thuot. The convoy's communication, if something happens, is our advisor net.

Next day, Y'Duc brings another "Yard" into our office. He is over six feet tall, thin, his middle-age face covered with stubble, barefoot and wearing the typical dark

On Our Own

Montagnard loincloth. An old, dirty, short-sleeved pullover shirt about four sizes too large covers his upper torso. He carries the small distinctive wooden ax that Montagnard men carry when traveling.

Y'Duc explains that the "Yard" was a soldier and NCO in the French Colonial Montagnard Division. Now he is Buon Brieng village chief, the large Montagnard village in the District's north, outside the artillery fan. A small palisade enclosed hamlet with the same name is also located inside the fan. He sleeps in this government controlled hamlet and returns to his village during daylight.

Speaking in broken French and Vietnamese, the Buon Brieng chief says that morning when going to his village he saw a large military force moving west to east. There were "beaucoup" soldiers and "sung coi" moving right inside the artillery fan.

The "sung coi," mortars, sound like 82-MM. Mortars this large will destroy our bunkers.

The Major, after hearing about the mortars, again tells Na Han that the bunkers need reinforcement with center beams, braces and standoffs.

That night the evening sky above Dat Hieu fills with tracers. Then slowly, the firing dies off, then ceases.

The Vietnamese hamlet radio net, an AM net using commercial Motorola radios with the District as the net control station, starts "squawking"

The Dat Hieu Popular Force report they caught someone trying to enter the hamlet over the palisade fence.

At first light the prisoner is brought to the District, a young khaki clad private from Regiment 18B. He became sick on the journey south and was left behind. Then he got lost trying to rejoin his unit. He climbed the hamlet wall to find help because his political commissar said everyone in the south welcomes the North Vietnamese Army. The Popular Force poor shooting saved his life. A helicopter takes him to Ban Me Thuot.

The weeks drag by, no more is heard of Regiment 18B. It vanishes.

Our War

Na Han, though, keeps the Popular Force busy laying squad size ambushes outside the perimeter at night and rebuilding bunkers in the daytime.

Dian first asks then taunts the Major to let him go out with the ambushes. He complains that the ambush parties are worthless. They walk out in the evening carrying blankets, their boots untied. All they are doing is disappearing from sight and then putting in "booby traps" before going to sleep.

The "booby traps" are C-ration cans staked beside a trail. A grenade, its safety pin removed, is placed in the can. The C-ration can, slightly larger than a grenade, holds the grenade's firing pin handle in place once the safety pin is removed. Attached to the grenade is a taut wire running across the trail staked into the ground on the other side. Anyone coming down the trail will hit the wire pulling the grenade from the can, popping the handle, exploding the grenade. Once the "booby traps" are in, the ambush party sleeps.

The Major refuses all requests.

I have my own problems. On payday I get neither money nor my "pink" slip, the Army form given every soldier on payday showing his pay breakdown. Almost all my pay goes by allotment to my wife in the States. With three kids, she lives month to month on an Army Captain's pay.

After the others receive their "pink" slips but I do not, I catch the next helicopter to Ban Me Thuot. The payroll clerk there tells me that my "pink" slip was not received from Saigon. He thinks that since I was assigned first to Pleiku it went there and assures me that the allotment to my wife had gone through and she will be paid.

A few days later my wife's letter tells me she was not paid.

Proper Army procedure is to go up the chain of command through Ban Me Thuot and have them find out why no pay. But wanting my wife paid this lifetime, I write to the Inspector General (IG) in Saigon. It gets results; my wife gets her allotment. In turn the IG sends me a letter saying it was my fault she was not paid; the Army never screws

On Our Own

up!

I also need money for travel. I am to go to Saigon for an orientation for advisors on how to deal with the many United States Agencies.

I fly to Saigon, hitching a ride from Ban Me Thuot on Air America, jokingly called "Air Nuc-Mam" from its ever-pervading stench on the C-47's.

Saigon hotels are expensive but I find a cheap, new one off Tu Do Street, a few blocks from the school. A building boom is going on. Hotels are needed to house all the Americans now arriving, both government employees and businessmen vying to sell goods to the Vietnamese

With no weapons allowed, I turn my carbine in at the MP check-in point across from the Brinks hotel.

I continue to pack a small .22 caliber Beretta that Powers lends me.

Luckily, I never need it. After returning to the District Powers and I test fire the pistol; the barrel cracks on the first shot. He tells me it is no big loss. He paid five dollars for it to a stranger in the Ban Me Thuot hotel lobby.

Now adjusted to the heat, I enjoy my time in Saigon, eating at the various French restaurants, hitting the bars and massage parlors, relaxing.

After what seems like a week R&R, I am back at District.

Returning finds nothing changed.

As soon as I return Dian tells me he is going to Ban Me Thuot and file a complaint with Ireland about the Major.

During my absence, the 1st Cav showed up in the District. The Cav fought Regiment 18B down on the coastal plain. For several weeks, at night, we could see the explosions from the artillery illuminating the sky. Now the Cav is on the regiment's trail, hoping to finish it—if it can find it.

A battalion from the Cav moved into the District.

Our War

What upsets Dian was the Major's response when the Cav battalion intelligence officer (S-2) asked what information we had on Regiment 18B.

We had no reports on the regiment since early June. Yet the Major tells the S-2 he has good information on its location, sending the Cav on a wild goose chase to the north. The troops are lifted-in based on the Major's report. As the information is a figment of the Major's imagination, the Cav hits nothing.

I tell Dian to clam down. Province is already wary about the Major.

It is not hard for me to believe that the Major did this. I have heard similar tales from officers on the Province staff.

I bunk with Captains on the Province staff when in Ban Me Thuot.

They despise the Major. When there he constantly complains about the Province staff. At the same time he spreads tales that the District is extremely dangerous with constant Viet Cong contact.

In reality, we have no enemy activity except for shots fired by nervous Popular Force soldiers in the outlying hamlets at night.

The Cav visit also caused another problem. Its enlisted men were in bad shape, having lived in the field for several months. Their clothes were ripped, torn or missing; the troopers traveling so light that they had no sleeping gear.

One platoon spent a night in the compound. The American soldiers were so miserable that Dian borrowed ponchos from the Regional Force Company so the Cav soldiers could have some cover sleeping that night. The next day the platoon left taking the ponchos with them.

Now the Regional Force Company commander asks me to get the ponchos back. By then the battalion is long gone. I tell the company commander that the Cav is gone and I do not know when I can get the ponchos back. The Lieutenant gives me a sad smile saying he understands; he will tell his men that the "The ponchos have been borrowed for a long, long time!"

On Our Own

Life is peaceful. There seems to be an unwritten agreement that as long as the District keeps its forces within the artillery fan, the Viet Cong will stay outside. Na Han likes this arrangement. It avoids bad reports. No enemy contact makes it look like the District is under firm government control.

Every few months I fill out a report on the hamlets in the District. It is Defense Secretary McNamara's new management tool to show "light at the end of the tunnel."

The Hamlet Evaluation Report is designed to reflect the success of the so-called "Ink blot" process, where, from a central location, the government slowly spreads, like an "Ink blot," to control the countryside.

One reason for the orientation in Saigon was to learn how to fill out this report. We spent hours on its concept.

An automated report, formatted for keypunching with objective questions containing multi-guess answers, once completed in pencil at District it goes to Saigon where the data is key punched and entered into an IBM computer. The computerized output reflects the war's successful progress.

Creativity goes into filling it out. The object is to give answers so that when things turn sour there is wiggle-room to show future progress. At the same time the current report needs to show the District under control with the advisors doing a great job.

My initial report shows most of the District population living within the controlled area. But it also reflects that more assistance needs to be given to cover the whole District with the "Ink blot." Wiggle room is left for subsequent reports to show the "Ink blot" spreading, even if we do nothing.

Though told the reports will not be used for evaluating advisors, everyone knows the Army's natural tendency to use any report as a "report card" in writing Officer Efficiency Reports. Besides, no one wants headquarters asking why we are not doing our job in spreading the "Ink blot."

Our War

Like all computer generated statistical report, garbage in equals garbage out.

The Major does not mind Na Han's arrangement limiting military activity.

The Major wants to avoid any action that endangers us.

Having survived the vicious fight at the Pusan perimeter and the disastrous retreat from the Yalu, he does not trust our egocentric politicians. To him this war dreamed up by Kennedy's academic eggheads to show a resolute President is not worth dying in.

I share the Major's attitude.

Seeing Kennedy's pancake make-up covered face when passing in review at his inauguration clued me that he was a phony. I am not surprised when he rolls over on the Bay of Pigs, Berlin wall, or Cuban Missiles.

For the Major dying to protect an ineffective dead politician's reputation is not in his nor, if he can help it, our future.

His concerns are improving his creature comforts until he returns stateside and his business in Texas costing him a small fortune each month.

But, excepting Bearfoot, the rest, young, none thinking about dying but rather hoping to enjoy an exciting adventure, want to conduct military operations, take a walk in the sun, smell gunpowder. Life in the compound is dull: reading books, playing volleyball, repairing bunkers, and answering government correspondence.

To the Major the knowledge that those under him do not share his view irritates and angers.

Also I do not trust him. Our strange first meeting made me leery. What remaining confidence I have is soon lost by his erratic behavior towards me. When we went on the District tour, he told me to drive the jeep. Unfamiliar with the four-wheel drive gears, I have trouble getting it in gear. Telling me to get out, he gets behind the steering wheel saying, to the enlisted men standing there, that I am not to drive any vehicles. I am embarrassed and mad.

On Our Own

A few days later some minor bureaucrats from the Agency for International Development (USAID) visit. The Major takes them by jeep to inspect a fortified "New Life" hamlet. Parking at the gate he walks into the hamlet leaving his carbine in the jeep. In the hamlet, he turns and asks me, "Where's my carbine." I tell him "In the jeep where you left it." His face turns red and he explodes in front of the visitors yelling at me for not bringing it, as if he expects me to carry it. He then orders me to get it. I say nothing, it is an order. I amble back and fetch it.

This is my last trouble with the man. After that he lets me have my way, but the damage is done. I do not trust him.

Nor do I trust Dian.

A friendless man, he says what he feels often rubbing salt into wounded spirits. Saying he is unafraid to die, perhaps because he looks upon it as a great release from life's inner turmoil, he acts as if he enjoys and embraces danger.

When the report came of Regiment 18B moving through the District, Dian wanted to move out with a small patrol to establish contact and monitor their moves. Even though something more than shooting artillery at a trail picked off a map, it is a quixotic gesture considering our capability.

I fear that by egging the Major on he will endanger us all by getting us involved in something stupid. War to him may meet a personal need; I do not know. While the rest want to enjoy the adventure, we all want to go home; he does not.

I do know that the growing antagonism between him and the Major worries me. The Major's focus on avoiding losing his shirt in his business while passing his year in as much comfort as possible until he gets stateside and retires infuriates Dian.

He insinuates the Major's inaction is from cowardice.

The Major retaliates by telling everyone who listens (other than Dian) that Dian is a gutless queer.

The anger between them burdens the whole team's relation. Even the evening game of "Hearts" is now vicious with the Major and Dian arguing over the play with the

Our War

intensity one expects when money is bet.

Resupply fuels more animosity.

The helicopters providing weekly supplies are replaced by a section of fixed wing "Bird-dogs" which lack the payload to carry our supplies. We feel lucky if a "Bird-dog" flies out to the District once or twice a week, buzzes our location like a "Stuka" dive-bomber, then drops a sandbag stuffed with official correspondence and mail. "Sorry 'bout that" radio the pilots when the drop as often as not lands in the barbed wire and not the compound.

If we yell on the radio enough, Province borrows a helicopter every few weeks from Pleiku that lands loaded with gasoline, propane, and potable water. To get American food a team member hitches a ride in on a "Birddog" or chopper, hoping to find a ride back after he buys the food from the Ban Me Thuot mess hall. Everything, drinking water, food, gas, or other necessities like beer, is flown in by helicopter or comes up Highway 14 in the few and far between convoys.

Highway 14 is coded red. The Viet Cong can set an ambush along any stretch when the mood strikes them. Military use is limited to convoys. But Vietnamese civilians regularly use the highway paying taxes if stopped by a Viet Cong tax unit—civilian trucks travel daily between Pleiku and Ban Me Thuot. Seeing the civilian traffic on the highway, the Major talks about using the highway to travel regularly into Ban Me Thuot.

With no side controlling the highway, luck determines whether you meet the Viet Cong. Chance determines life and death. Combat is all about luck. Napoleon asked "Is he lucky?" when selecting Generals.

Before my arrival, the Major drove the highway to Ban Me Thuot. Placing four Montagnards with BAR's in the jeep trailer and two more in the back seat, and keeping a FM PRC-25 radio on an open channel with both the District and Province, he flew the twenty five miles to Ban Me Thuot. Nothing happened.

On Our Own

The Major figures if he can do it once we can do it on a regular/irregular basis.

Not getting his daily mail is driving him nuts. In Texas his $50,000 grader sits idle while he sits on a hill in Vietnam making payments. He wants to know how the business is doing. Yet each time he hears, he gets more morose; the news is never good. But no news is worst. He wants daily mail delivery, but our District is not on any postman's route.

He wants us to drive to Ban Me Thuot to pick up his mail.

No one wants to run the road to pick up mail. To the rest of us mail is nice to get, though none get any regularly.

I am not getting much nor do I expect to. My wife is pregnant with our fourth child. She is not happy that I left for the war.

If beer or food are needed, the trip may be worth putting your life on the line—but not for a nonexistent letter.

The Major and Bearfoot make a few trips. Bearfoot's Vietnamese woman lives in Ban Me Thuot.

The Major badgers Dian into the trip, insinuating he is a coward if he does not go.

Stedman and Powers go; danger never enters their young minds. It is a game.

Finally, I make the trip to reach the airfield in Ban Me Thuot to catch Air America for school in Saigon.

Travel on the hard top is reasonably safe.

The war is taking a vacation. It is the planting season. In the highlands, the field rice needs intensive labor. Even the Viet Cong work the fields. Those that remain with their units have a hard time. Little rice is left to levy before the next harvest.

It is also the monsoon season. Heavy rains come in the late afternoon, pouring an hour or so, turning the red clay into a deep mud making movement arduous. It is too

Our War

miserable for military activity. Only after the harvest in November and December will activity start up.

The trip is routine, but we are angry with the Major for putting our lives on the line for his mail.

The Major and Bearfoot after making a run return saying Ireland rotated; our new Province advisor is Lieutenant Colonel Monroe.

The next day, Bearfoot's Ban Me Thuot whore shows up in a Lambretta loaded with her bedding and other possessions. Unloading, she moves into Bearfoot's sleeping bunker.

The Major announces she is now our cook.

Each of us contributes money monthly for our joint mess paying for soft drinks, beer and food. Her salary will come from this.

Dian is furious. The day she arrives he tells me while we are standing by the administration building that she had been the cook but left after he complained to Ireland. Ireland told the Major to fire her.

Dian does not want to pay for Bearfoot's pleasure. He rages that Bearfoot is "so horny he will screw a snake," saying Bearfoot tried to put the make on women in the compound. He hustled a Vietnamese Sergeant's wife and barely escaped with his life when the husband's pistol shot missed.

Angrily he tells me that he is going to the new Province advisor if the woman stays.

I tell Dian to hold up, I will talk to the Major. I am concerned. Though homely, she is still a woman and we are six men. That arithmetic adds up to trouble.

Getting the Major alone, I make clear to him that Dian and I do not want Bearfoot's woman here. She has to go; she is trouble.

The Major is upset, arguing that Bearfoot is our cook and if he cannot have the woman, he will transfer to Ban Me Thuot. Finally, he realizes he has no option but to tell her to go.

On Our Own

The next day, Bearfoot's woman packs, loads her bed on the Lambretta and leaves. A few months later I hear from a Province advisor that she was arrested for smuggling medicine to the Viet Cong.

Bearfoot transfers to Ban Me Thuot within the week.

FIRST OPERATION

Na Han, upset, walks into our office to announce he is going to run an operation.

A young Vietnamese cow-herder from Dat Hieu was stabbed to death on the trail to old Dat Hieu, an abandoned hamlet. Some Vietnamese are still staying there. Na Han believes they are Viet Cong or sympathizers. The hamlet is about 10 kilometers northwest, within the artillery fan.

Two Buon Trieng Popular Force platoons stay in the compound that evening. Buon Trieng is Catholic so the platoons are politically reliable. They recently returned from the training center at Ban Me Thuot, and are equipped with new uniforms, including boots carried in their rucksacks—the boots hurt their feet—and World War II weapons, M-1's and carbines—rather than obsolete shotguns and 1903s.

Na Han locks them in the compound for the night, insuring they will be here in the morning. It also prevents loose tongues. In the evening after the gates are closed the Popular Force are told we are going to old Dat Hieu.

There is no building for the PF to sleep in; they camp out in the compound courtyard. Their chatter keeps me awake. I feel as if I just fell asleep when at five in the morning the compound comes to life.

For breakfast, with no cooking facilities, the PF eat compacted rice balls wrapped in green leaves stored in their boot socks.

The plan calls for us to leave at six but confusion and disorganization delays departure until seven thirty.

Our War

Radio calibration problems, arguments about command and last minute instructions delay us. The Regional Force radios, PRC-10's, must be calibrated with the compound radios, as well as those in each platoon. "Mot, hai, ba..." is repeated over and over as they try to get them aligned.

Stedman is carrying the advisor radio, a newer PRC-25 radio with greater range that requires no calibration.

Eventually the Regional Force radio operators give up and we go.

The column consists of the Regional Force company and two Montagnard platoons from the compound as well as the two platoons from Buon Trieng. Also along are some District staff with Powers, and Stedman and I.

The column walks out of the compound gate, takes a left across the ridge running to the north and, following back trails, meanders towards old Dat Hieu.

Shortly before noon we arrive.

No one is there. The troops in the column fan out, sit down and eat lunch. The Buon Trieng Popular Force finish off the rice ball remains in their socks.

Trees lining the small stream that runs through the hamlet's ruins give us shade.

Lieutenant Long, the always grinning Civil Affairs officer responsible for running the Popular Force in the District, sits next to me. He tells me he was assigned to old Dat Hieu when he first came from Saigon. His job was to make the hamlet a "New Life" hamlet. Several times the Viet Cong came in the evening to kill him. He escaped by hiding in the stream we are sitting next to, breathing through a straw until they left.

Those peasants who supported the government eventually moved to new Dat Hieu located on Highway 14 north of the District compound.

Looking around, I can see that most of the thatched houses are collapsed and abandoned though some look as if lived in. The fields are planted.

After an hour break, the column starts back.

Some Vietnamese are met on the trail. Sergeant Y'Duc questions them. They say they were working at the Mewal plantation and now are going home; they are

On Our Own

released.

Na Han is upset. No enemy contact, then Vietnamese on the trail where they should not be, none kept as prisoners. He wants a rerun but not right now.

SFC Bozilov, Bearfoot's replacement, transfers in.

Born in Bulgaria, Bozilov was wounded crossing the Danube with the Russian Army in World War II. He fled into Greece in 1949, during the troubles on the Bulgarian—Greek boarder, and then like many European displaced persons, volunteered for the American Army.

A characteristic Slav, he is untouched by confusing western liberal sentimentality. Hard bodied and hard headed, but with shrewd peasant intelligence, though outwardly polite and obsequious to those in authority, inwardly he is contemptuous and independent: an excellent infantryman.

Bozilov tells the Major he is an infantry Sergeant not a cook. As the ranking NCO, his solution to the cook situation is to elevate the Montagnard Popular Force soldier given us by Na Han as a houseboy to cook.

Y'Non, the houseboy, is a boy in name only. Less than five feet tall, his erect thin little body struts around the compound at one slow speed, his wizen face lighted with a constant grin. His age is indeterminate. A former soldier with the French Colonial Montagnard Division, he had been at the Special Forces camp at Buon Brieng when the Montagnards rebelled and killed their Vietnamese officers.

Y'Non is not high in the Montagnard social order. He was designated by Y'Don the compound's Montagnard Popular Force chief to do menial tasks for us that are normally done by women such as laundry or carrying water. Bo-didly or Bo as we nickname Y'Non, smilingly, though slowly and slovenly, does them.

His initial cooking skills are nonexistent, requiring constant supervision. Luckily, we all like spicy foods. Traditional Montagnard cooking means cook anything and then spice it with small, hot, red and green peppers.

Our War

After some basic instruction on American canned food, Bo prepares an edible meal. Sanitation remains beyond his grasp. But he accepts our idiosyncrasies, particularly after Bozilov turns purple with rage, screaming when something is not scrubbed clean.

Like any soldier on special duty in any army, Bo gets himself excused from all details such as guard, night ambushes or operations.

Bo also receives some cash and our leftover food, a significant addition to his 300 "P's" monthly Popular Force pay and 100-pound rice sack.

The PF's pay is not a living wage. It is suppose to supplement the income from the crops raised by him in his hamlet's fields. With possible death for the Montagnards living in the compound to work their outlying fields, USAID gives them a 100 pound rice sack in addition to their 300 "P's" pay. Even with the rice, it is hard to feed a large family.

In time Bo exploits his position to become the intermediary between the Montagnards and the Americans. Bo's access to our meat scraps gives him influence with the other Montagnards.

Meat is hard to get; any scrap is valuable. One day while walking around the compound I notice a Regional Force Sergeant cooking some small pieces of meat on a spit over an open fire. As I walk over to see what he has, the Sergeant raises his head, smiles, giving the universal sign that he is about to have a sumptuous meal by rubbing his stomach. Walking closer I see that he is roasting two large rats. I smile and walk away.

As long as we have our interpreters, Nguyen and Dong around, Bo's slow, strutting walk around the compound amuses. But when the interpreters are gone, as they are more and more, Bo's "pidgin" French, Rhade and English are how we communicate with the Montagnards. When we need some laborers to work on a project, Bo with his "pidgin" talk gets them. They are happy for the work, we pay with food. Bo eventually is giving orders to the Popular Force camp leader as the American's voice. His strutting walk begins to reflect, at least in his eyes, his importance.

On Our Own

As Bo's skills progress, Bozilov loses interest in the kitchen, other than keeping it supplied with American food.

Bearfoot traveled regularly to Ban Me Thuot to buy food from the MACV mess. Shortly after joining us, Bozilov runs the jeep to Ban Me Thuot to buy rations.

One job that the advisor team in Ban Me Thuot has is logistic support for our District. We buy our rations from their mess. The mess in Ban Me Thuot picks up rations at the quartermaster ration breakdown point in Nah Trang, convoying the rations up from the coast each Thursday.

The Ban Me Thuot mess officer was selling us rations at the same price they were charged in Nah Trang.

A new Lieutenant Colonel now runs the Ban Me Thuot MACV mess. He decides to add a surcharge on the rate charged us, rather than charging the price the government sells the rations to him.

He tells Bozilov we are not entitled to the mess rate since we are not located with them. The surcharge is a profit for the Ban Me Thuot mess to spend as they see fit. That means buying goodies for the senior officers.

Bozilov objects. He argues Ban Me Thuot is our higher headquarters, their job is to support us, not make a profit by gouging us. The Colonel remains firm. Bozilov angrily buys the food for the price asked.

This price gouging upsets the whole team. During the weeks after Bozilov's return, we prepare for our return to Ban Me Thuot when food runs low.

Through Bo we put out word that we are in the market for Montagnard cross bows, musical instruments, pipes and knives. Crude and handmade, the Montagnards are mass-producing them for the GI tourist trade.

Once word is out, Montagnards start coming into the District compound and squat in front of our office waiting to negotiate a deal for the artifacts.

So many are selling crossbows that I organize a shoot off to determine which to

Our War

buy.

Acting as middlemen, we buy crossbows and other trinkets for a few hundred "P." If needed we can barter them for twenty times their cost with the MACV mess personnel in Ban Me Thuot. Americans want to take a crossbow back to the states.

I also read the rules in the *Army Handbook*. I am confident that reason will prevail and I can convince the Colonel to eliminate the surcharge on our purchases.

With food low, Dian, Bozilov and I drive to Ban Me Thuot.

No argument works with the Colonel. He wants his surcharge. All of us are pissed. We stay overnight.

I go to the Province advisors. They laugh. Any surcharge we pay benefits them as Ban Me Thuot MACV mess members. I cannot believe that the Army officers in Ban Me Thuot would try to chisel us, but they do

That night, I drink myself silly in the officers club.

The club is a bar with some tables in a long room in Bao Dai's palace. The bartender is a NCO I know who works at Province.

To preclude any skimming by the bartender, a chit book must be purchased. All drinks are paid for with chits. I throw the chit book on the bar. The bartender takes one, giving me a drink. During the rest of the evening he takes more chits, constantly refilling my glass. After sleeping in someone's bunk who is in the field, I wake with a slight hangover, chits worth forty cents missing from the book.

At breakfast, Bozilov and Dian tell me they talked at the NCO club to the mess Sergeant. The mess Sergeant is willing to trade food for the Montagnard trinkets.

I do not want to trade with the mess Sergeant. We will be at his mercy. I tell them to give me one more chance and go back to the Colonel hoping that as a reasonable man he will change his mind. He is adamant. No persuasion works. He is one of the clerk types that the Army attracts in peacetime; his goal is pleasing his boss.

My inbred Irish anger against those who abuse authority, the natural result from English persecution for centuries, takes over. Finding Bozilov and Dian, I tell them to go

60

ahead and deal with the mess Sergeant.

Later that day, Bozilov and Dian pull up behind the mess hall with the jeep and trailer and barter for the food. We return to District with the jeep trailer full.

The Colonel eventually realizes something is going on. Several times he sees us leaving with a full trailer, yet there is no records of payment. He becomes particularly upset after finding us one afternoon in his storeroom looking over rations. After that he keeps a close watch over the exits to the mess hall, yet catches no one. Others in the Ban Me Thuot compound gets a kick out of the Colonel's frustration and runs interference for us; besides they want our trinkets.

The problem with the mess officer introduces me to Gerry Brown, an easy going Texan, who has my job in An Loc, the District located between Ban Me Thuot and ours. It is the other MACV advised District in the Province. Since the surcharge also applies to An Loc, we try together to get the mess officer to change his mind. He never does.

This barter system has one great drawback. We can trade only for food that the mess Sergeant has excess, food he scrounged and does not show on his records.

Frozen government meat rations come in fifty-pound packs. For some reason the mess Sergeant has a super excess of spare ribs. Our propane refrigerator is too small to keep all fifty pounds frozen. As soon as we return, they are smoked. Spare ribs get tiring after the first hundred pounds.

The mess hall also has an abundant supply of SPAM; luckily Powers loves it and eats all we get.

SECOND OPERATION

Na Han decides it is time for the rerun to old Dat Hieu.

The Popular Force are brought in the night before, the gates locked, orders issued—a restless nights sleep with the Popular Force jabbering away all night—then early awake, disorganization, confusion and finally by six thirty, we go.

Our War

To gain surprise the column will move north on Highway 14 before going to Dat Hieu. The artillery platoon's two 2 1/2 ton trucks and the District's 2 1/2 ton are squeezed full, over fifty soldiers jammed into each. Wherever there is any space on the trucks there is a body including several standing on the running board and seating on the front fenders. Bozilov, Powers, Stedman and I go with them. With bodies hanging all over the trucks, there is no room for us. Dian drives us in the jeep.

The gates are opened, the trucks go down the hill to Highway 14, and then turn left barreling north up the highway to the outer limits of District control.

Quickly dismounting, we all enter the woods. The trucks and jeep turn and go.

Captain Yee runs the operation. A Montagnard titled Inspector General of Popular Force, he is in his late thirties, slightly built, and always dressed in grubby, well worn "tiger" fatigues, his chin covered with gray stubble. He speaks English and French.

Several years before he was the District chief but lost the job after attacking and overrunning Con Diem, a Viet Cong controlled hamlet. Yee celebrated his victory by drinking himself senseless. When the Viet Cong counterattacked his troops left him when they retreated. Seeing his rigid body, the Viet Cong thought him dead, saving his life. Valuing this lesson he has since remained constantly intoxicated.

Before starting out the gate on this operation Na Han walks over and opens Yee's canteen to check that he is carrying only water. Yee enjoys nam-pay, the Montagnard home brew. Today he is sober.

Yee is in charge because both the Regional Force company and the Truong Son company are going.

Truong Son are Montagnards recruited by the CIA, trained in company size units, uniformed in "tiger" fatigues and heavily armed with automatic World War II weapons (M-2 carbines and Thompson submachine guns). Their job is to provide protection for Montagnard hamlets undergoing Rural Development, the current word choice by Saigon indicating government presence in a Montagnard Buon.

On Our Own

Saigon constantly introduces new government programs to increase its influence with the peasants.

In theory, as practiced in Saigon, the government programs "Rural Development," "New Life," "Rural Reconstruction," are different. At the District level what happens remains the same. You concentrate the population into a small living area then build bunkers and palisades around that area. At the same time recruit and arm a Popular Force unit; give the population rice, cooking oil, and other USAID goods for a few months; and put in a health care worker, public affairs, and some police presence. Then, with this Buon designated secure, the Truong Son move on to another Buon and provide security for it until it also is brought under government control.

The CIA trains and controls the Truong Son units, perhaps because the "Rural Development" program goal is to weed out the Viet Cong supporters. Whatever the reason there are over a hundred well armed men in the District that the District chief cannot touch unless he gets permission from the CIA agents in Ban Me Thuot.

Two CIA agents living in downtown Ban Me Thuot pay, supply, and control the Truong Son

Downtown Ban Me Thuot, once the summer residence for well to do French and upper class Vietnamese, is a smaller and nicer Saigon. But now the large hotel in the center, the restaurants, shops, businesses and large homes are showing the war's effect, decaying from poor maintenance and care.

An elderly Montagnard ARVN Captain works as liaison between the CIA in Ban Me Thuot and the Truong Son in the District. He is disabled; civilization's pressure and too much nam-pay playing havoc with his stomach. Any conversation with him revolves around his many medical operations. He avoids confrontation and always manages to disappear when you need him.

As a result using Truong Son in District operations requires that a team member go to Ban Me Thuot and talk with the CIA agents. They operate out of a large cement house a few blocks off Highway 14 near the town center.

Our War

The deal making is not easy, as the CIA does not want Truong Son used in military operations. The explanation given is that some bureaucrat in Saigon decided that was the way it was going to be.

At first, the local agents refusal is overcome with Johnny Walker, some beer, and gifts of Montagnard trinkets combined with the promise that they will not be asked again unless absolutely needed. As requests become more frequent, it becomes more and more difficult to obtain the agent's agreement. Even Johnny Walker fails to lubricate the wheels of cooperation.

The Truong Son District commander, who I know by the title "Chef de Camp," and referred to as "Le Chef," is an old campaigner. Serving in the French army, he withdrew with the French into Laos during the French retreat after the Japanese occupation. Then he served with the Japanese, Viet Minh and finally rejoined the French before becoming an ARVN. Now he works for the CIA. A Montagnard, after twenty-seven years in combat he has returned to his native District.

The "Chef de Camp's" assistant is Lieutenant Duc. Duc, half Montagnard, half Vietnamese, worked in the District in various political jobs before joining the Truong Son. Duc says he hates the Viet Cong, joining the Truong Son because the Viet Cong recently kidnapped his father. He is no relation to Warrant Officer Duc with the Regional Force company.

Both Ducs as well as the "Chef de Camp" are in the column.

Yee commands because Province refuses to let a Truong Son lead the operation. The "Chef de Camp", a Captain, outranks Lieutenant Thuyn, our Regional Force company commander.

Our dismounted column moves single file through thick brush and woods, finally spreading out and stopping in open woods for lunch. The food I have is a C-ration can of fruit stuck in one of my ammo pouches.

I do not use the U.S. Army issued backpack. It is a cumbersome and awkward piece of equipment that attaches to the load bearing harness and sits on your rear rump.

On Our Own

To take it off requires taking off and disconnecting the harness. The backpack was designed by a human engineering firm to reduce stress on the back. No one considered that an infantryman in a fire fight wants to unload his pack fast. When overnight in the field, ruck sacks traded from Special Forces or the smaller Vietnamese version obtained by buying or borrowing are used.

Yee seeing I have only the fruit offers me some rice and canned sardines from his pack that a Popular Force soldier is carrying.

Warrant Officer Duc walks up. Excited, he tells us we will have a contact today. Last night he dreamed about a monkey, a sure sign.

The column starts again, over 150 men, single file. We move from the thickets and start crossing small clearings planted by Montagnards using slash and burn techniques. The troops cross the fields picking and eating everything edible like locust.

Finally the column reaches a hill by old Dat Hieu.

The hill blocks our view.

Yee detaches the Truong Son, ordering them to go around to old Dat Hieu's rear and set up a blocking position. Once they are in position, our column will push into the hamlet driving everyone towards them.

Having an attacking unit drive the enemy into a blocking force is not original. But as George Armstrong Custer discovered at the Little Big Horn, it has drawbacks. The split forces can be defeated in detail. We believe, however, the same as Custer thought about the Sioux, that the Viet Cong will run rather then stand and fight.

The Truong Son move off; a half-hour passes, then they radio they are in position.

Our column moves over the crest. The hamlet is on the opposite slope. A steep valley is to our front. The small, fast flowing, fordable stream runs through the trees at the valley's bottom. The column swings into line and we walk abreast across an open field down towards the stream.

The Truong Son are not in position. As we move over the crest I see them to

Our War

our north, on line, moving parallel across the fields. There is no blocking force, anything hit will escape.

From the hilltop I see a young Vietnamese couple walking hand in hand in the field to the Truong Son front. A peasant is working in the fields to our front on the opposite slope, about 500 meters away.

We have surprise.

Our line starts down the forward slope. I find myself looking down to avoid stepping in the punji stake holes on the hillside. I lose sight of the Truong Son.

Shots are fired on the other side of the valley.

The peasant looking up sees us. I raise my carbine and fire a burst; the range is too far. With the bullets flying in a high arc, I do not have enough mix of tracer with ball to adjust on him. He runs up the slope over the crest and disappears. (After this I increase my tracer mix to one tracer for every three ball rounds; hopefully it will let me adjust on the target no matter what the range.)

The line picks up speed as everyone wants to leave the open slope and reach cover in the trees by the stream. Moving through the tree line at the bottom, the Regional Force company opens fire.

A small trail runs from the tree line across the stream up to the crest on the opposite slope; on it four men are running flat out—this is where the Truong Son are suppose to be but are not—the men reach the crest and go over. The Regional Force company drops a 60-MM mortar round on the crest in frustration. The Viet Cong are gone; no one is blocking.

I call District on the PRC-25 Stedman is carrying. The Regional Force equipped with their obsolete PRC-10's, whether from poor maintenance, old batteries, poor calibration or terrain, are blocked from transmitting to District.

The advisors can talk to each other. It dawns on me that I can pretty much control what goes on since I have the only radio that can reach anyone outside our column.

On Our Own

Several huts in the abandoned hamlet have been rebuilt since our last visit. The Regional Force company commander orders his soldiers to burn them. The ten or so newly rebuilt thatched huts are torched and soon in flames.

I am standing with the advisor team by a burning hut when suddenly three women and two children burst from the thick brush, about twenty feet away, screaming and crying.

A Regional Force Sergeant tells me that the women are yelling that a child is in the burning hut.

The soldiers look at the women but do nothing, telling me it may be a booby-trap. The women continue to squeal, yell, cry, and then fall moaning by the burning hut.

Bozilov and Powers each grab a long bamboo pole and using the pole start pulling the hut apart. Warrant Officer Duc and some of the Popular Force help; the women continue to sit on the ground wailing and moaning. In a few minutes, the thatched hooch is pulled apart.

One of the women, continuing to wail, runs over to a small bunker in the hut's back. Reaching in she pulls out a small boy, about four years old. He is untouched.

While pulling the hooch apart Powers noticed that the ground in front feels funny when walked on. It is soft and neatly raked, not beaten hard like the ground around it.

Captain Yee orders the Popular Force to dig up the ground. Pots, pans, plates and silverware (the Vietnamese use both chopsticks and silverware) are uncovered. Enough to feed a platoon. The items are destroyed.

Yee thinks this is a way station between Mewal and the north.

Taking the women and children, the column moves back up the slope we walked down.

The Major wants to give the artillery gunners some training. For the next hour, the Vietnamese, use our radio adjusting artillery, demolishing the abandoned hamlet.

Our War

Meantime the Major obtains a plane by telling Province that the column is in contact. With our airstrip now approved, the Major hitches a ride at District and soon is overhead in the "Bird-dog."

While our forward observer adjusts the artillery, the troops spread out and sit down along a trail on the bare slope above the hamlet.

The plane flies slowly back and fourth making passes trying to locate us. Neither the Major nor the pilot spot us. I give directions over the radio. They continue to bore holes, not seeing us. Over 150 people sit in the open waving madly. Eventually, after six or seven unsuccessful passes, I throw a smoke grenade. This they spot.

If a slow moving "Bird-dog" cannot find a highly visible target trying to be found, how can jet pilots find targets that do not want to be found on the Ho Chi Minh trail?

After making several more passes, the plane departs. Our column starts to the compound, the women screaming and dragging themselves along.

The afternoon sun beats down on us. After walking a few hundred meters my uniform is soaked from sweat. During a brief halt at a stream to refill canteens the heat turns my green fatigues white from the dried salt.

Everyone is tired and suffering from the heat. The Regional Force company commander wants to take an easy route on the main trail to District. Since we had contact I fear that the Viet Cong will anticipate that. I suggest to Yee that he lead us down a steep trail, wade the river, and go up the opposite side on another steep path rather then cross the ford.

A heavy downpour begins as the column starts, turning the trail to mud. The column moves fast leaving the women and children on the trail. Na Han does not want them; he will have to feed them.

On Our Own

Rossi plantation main building.

Our War

L-19 landing on the strip the Major built.

On Our Own

The daily volleyball game in front of the District headquarters.

Taking a break on one of our walks. The thick canopy precludes growth at ground level, which makes walking easy as long as not crossing a river or swamp.

On Our Own

Going to town. PF's with BAR's loading in the trailer

Our War

CHAPTER FOUR

Congress mandates that the American military insure that weapons and equipment given to foreign nations are properly accounted for and maintained. This is used as a legal fiction to permit American advisors to fight with the Vietnamese, the weapons users.

The *Army Handbook* directs advisors to inspect the Popular Force equipment twice a year. The Major agrees with me that the best way to do this is to accompany the paymaster. Though Na Han recruits, supplies and controls the Popular Force in the District, he does not pay them. The paymaster comes from Province.

The Province paymaster goes every month to the hamlets and pays each Popular Force soldier. The soldier shows up with his identification card and signs on the muster roll that he received his pay. Every soldier can be counted to show up on payday. The District rolls show almost 1800.

While with the paymaster I notice that the pay given the soldiers does not include a pay raise I read about in a MACV information letter.

I ask Lieutenant Long why the Popular Force are not receiving the raise. As the District officer who runs the Popular Force he should know.

Giving me the quizzical look that he often does when he cannot understand why I ask a question when the answer is obvious, he explains, "This is the first month for the new pay, Dai-wy. This month money goes to officers who get raise for Popular Force. Next month soldiers get theirs."

Often in the evening, Na Han, becoming more familiar with us, spends time visiting, drinking our cold beer. That evening, while sitting around the dining table in the office sipping beer, I ask him about the Popular Force pay explanation given me by Long.

Na Han responds that what Long said is true. He then adds that as District chief he could make more money but is not interested in making too much. That would mean hurting people in the District. His yearly government salary is 15,000 Piasters and, though tempted, his total income is not more than 50,000 Piasters a year.

Living And Learning

He tells us that it is understood that if you want something from the government, a small gift is in order.

As we all know indirect bribes are legal in the States. Most payoffs' are through campaign contributions although sometimes other methods are used such as a contractor hiring a mayor's husband as a "consultant" in order to get a redevelopment contract or a business retaining a law firm in which the governor's wife is a partner. Commonly, non-tax paying organizations hire a politician's child or other relative to insure getting government grants.

In Vietnam, though, payments are upfront; you pay for services given. Na Han gives us an example, telling about a woman whose ARVN husband was killed. He obtained a 20,000 Piasters pension for her. In gratitude she gave him 2000.

Na Han lives frugally. Of his two small rooms one is used as a kitchen and sleeping area for his two Jerai bodyguards. The other has a table, two chairs and Na Han's bed. If getting wealthy, he is salting it away somewhere else.

The problem with collecting graft is that the artificially supported Piaster has no value. Few consumer goods can be bought with Piasters on the open market.

The Vietnamese peasant's thatched hut usually contains a locally made bed, table with chairs, tea and cooking pot, dishes and eating utensils and some storage chests. Anything beyond that is a luxury item that the peasant will never see nor have the cash to buy.

Nor does everyone get access to the valuable goods the United States gives away through the various agencies, only those connected to the officials distributing them. Working for the Americans is the key to getting ahead; the Americans have the money and goods.

USAID has the most goods. USAID field workers, Koreans and Filipinos acting as super-clerks at Province, insure that receipts cover all goods given away.

At District, advisors get involved. Periodically USAID has rice, bulgur wheat

Our War

and cooking oil to give to the Popular Force. The oil is valuable—a can costs 1,000 Piasters on the black market.

This USAID program is for the Popular Force and does not include the Regional Force or ARVN. But some District officers think they should get a share.

Lieutenant Long and Sergeant Phong, the Popular Force supply Sergeant, are responsible for giving the USAID goods to the PF. They distribute them the same day they arrive. They will disappear if stored.

When the first cooking oil shipment arrives Sergeant Phong needs time to assemble the Popular Force. While he is doing this, the District officers climb into the truck carrying the oil and help themselves.

Phong knows he can do nothing with the officers. He leaves the crowd of Popular Force soldiers forming by the old District headquarters and comes up the compound hill to tell Bozilov.

Bozilov, as operations Sergeant, works closely with Phong monitoring the PF supplies. Bozilov goes ballistic as Phong begins telling him that the District officers are stealing the cooking oil.

Rushing from the office where we are sitting, Bozilov jumps into a jeep and speeds down the hill. At the bottom, seeing the District officers holding oil cans, he roars at them to return them. (The bulgur wheat and American rice also on the trucks are not an issue; they are not part of the Vietnamese diet. No one wants them.)

The officers, led by Lieutenant Thieu, ignore him. No Sergeant tells Thieu what to do.

Then Na Han, brought by the Major, arrives. He orders them to return the oil. They do. If there is such a thing as face, the officers have lost it.

Repercussions soon come.

A week later Phong tells me Province has ordered him transferred to Ban Me Thuot. While most in the compound would jump at the chance to live to Ban Me Thuot, Phong's home is in the District. He lives with his family outside the wire in a very large

Living And Learning

well-built wooden house (well he is the supply Sergeant!).

Powers and Stedman are particularly upset. Phong, they believe, is the Vietnamese type we should support, energetic and fairly honest. He is also their friend. Stedman obtained some Vietnamese/English language books from the United States Information Services (USIS) and has been teaching English to several District staff. Phong is his star pupil.

Though a military organization, our close living arrangement means everyone can express an opinion and influence what the team does. Stedman, Powers and Bozilov hammer on the Major to do something to stop the transfer.

Na Han refuses to do anything. His disingenuous excuse is that he can do nothing since Phong is Vietnamese.

The Major goes to the Province advisor; the transfer is canceled.

A convoy also brings a hundred unasked for cement bags for the Montagnard Popular Force in the compound.

Saigon bureaucrats decided that the Popular Force want cement houses. Cement and dirt are mixed and poured into a heavy cast iron mold that compresses the mixture into a building block by pressing down on a large metal handle. The block is then removed from the machine, and if it does not crumble, left to dry in the sun. The time consuming hand operated machine makes one brick at a time. There is one machine.

The Montagnard Popular Force soldiers want neither the bricks nor to waste time making them. Their elevated long houses in the Buons are wood. Wood is plentiful.

The machine is sent back to Ban Me Thuot.

Vietnamese want the cement—it is good trading material.

Some cement is traded to an ARVN Captain building a house in Ban Me Thuot for a jeep trailer. Our original trailer was stolen when the Major left it overnight outside the Ban Me Thuot MACV compound's front gate. The remaining cement is stored.

The District also receives American farming implements. No one wants these

Our War

strange tools.

USAID provides fertilizer too. The Vietnamese farmers use it but not the Montagnards.

Montagnards have no interest in fertilizer. They are slash and burn strip farmers, using the land for three or four years then moving on to another part of the forest. We often run across their small fields in the thick forest on operations.

Poor knowledge on fertilizer use is another reason. If a little fertilizer makes plants big, shouldn't throwing on a lot make them huge? There is an understandable reluctance to use it after crops are destroyed from over fertilizing.

Na Han decides who receives the USAID goods. He concludes no one will fault him if he does not give them away. The Americans cannot claim graft and neither the Vietnamese nor Montagnards can say he favors one group. He stores them in his padlocked warehouse by the old District headquarters.

The items sit in the warehouse. Due to the moisture in the air the remaining cement hardens, the tools rust, while the fertilizer remains unused.

Reluctantly, after much argument, Na Han releases the goods.

The remaining cement is loaned to an American Protestant Evangelical group in Ban Me Thuot building a church in the District. The agreement is for the church to replace it on demand, bag for bag.

The fertilizer goes to the Vietnamese. The farm implements, however, continue to rust away, no one wants them.

Also no one wants the Bulgur wheat, at least for food. It is not part of the diet. But the Vietnamese and Montagnards discover it makes a more potent alcoholic home brew than rice wine or nam-pay.

Nam-pay is not only an alcoholic drink to the Montagnards; it is a social event.

I am told that when two Montagnards meet the traditional greeting is "Nam-pay ruu" literally translated "let's get drunk together." That and "Yop ding hop," which I think translates to "Let's smoke a pipe," are the limits of my Montagnard. Entering an

78

Living And Learning

outlying Buon during our walks in the sun and saying these words gets a laugh from the headman. After that we are invited into his long house to sit drinking nam-pay, smoking our pipes, and talking "pidgin" French.

Nam-pay as far as I know requires no special skill to make. Yet there must be a secret, else everyone in the States would make it.

Somehow the Montagnards gets ordinary rice to ferment. They put a little rice in a tall earthenware open mouth jar and then place a cloth cover over the mouth to keep dirt out. It is let standing for a few days, or if really first rate nam-pay, up to three months.

When he has guests, the Montagnard sits his guests on hard wooden benches along the long house walls. He places the jar in the middle, removing the cloth cover and stuffing thick leaves from any nearby bush on the bottom of the jar. The jar is then filled with water, the leaves holding the rice in place at the bottom. Several hollowed out long straws that reach to the bottom are placed in the jar. Sucking on the straw, the same way you take gas from a car with an "Alabama credit card," the first couple of C-ration cans of water are siphoned off and thrown away. (Left over C- ration cans are multipurpose, besides being used for booby traps, they make excellent drinking cups and storage containers for small items.)

This first water is not very potent; more water than nam-pay, but it starts the process by mixing the water and rice. Then the straw is given to the guest of honor. The alcoholic content is highest at the beginning. Drinking commences by others from the other straws. After someone has enough he passes the straw to another guest. As the jar empties, more water is poured in, perhaps several times, with the straws passing back and forth until the nam-pay coming up the straw tastes more like water than alcohol. By then everyone feels good.

The Vietnamese and Montagnards also dislike the American rice. They complain that when cooked it does not stick together but is fluffy, tasteless and separates easily. Their rice is gooey and sticky, enabling them to roll it into balls and carry it easily

Our War

to the fields. The American rice is not wasted, like the bulgur wheat, it fuels the home brew industry.

Living And Learning

CPT. Yee demonstrating nam-pay to the radio relay Sergeant who is sipping on the straw from the jug.

Our War

CHAPTER FIVE

In Germany, the Air Force pilot assigned as the Brigade's forward air controller (FAC) remarked that flying was hours of sheer boredom interrupted by moments of stark terror. In the District, the war is boredom without the stark terror adrenaline high.

With no Viet Cong activity, life takes on a routine, uneventful existence.

The only break in the monotony is the excitement when an L-19 pilot flies into the strip every few days. They bring us the gossip from Ban Me Thuot and usually, in the back seat, besides mail, some beer, normally Hamms or Carlings Black Label or some other lesser known brand. The PX cannot keep "Bud" in supply.

The pilot's arrival is looked forward to; it enables us to get to Ban Me Thuot without using the road.

One pilot, Smith, I knew from Germany.

He had gone to flight school in route to Vietnam. Shortly after arriving in country he converted his "Bird-dog" into a "Stuka" mounting 2.35-inch rocket pods on the wings. A frustrated "Red Baron," now he is trying to figure out how to mount a machine gun without tearing off the wings or clipping his propeller.

The L-19 reconnaissance flights have no fixed flight pattern and the pilots generally spend their time flying aimlessly out over the border boring holes in the sky.

The Major uses their availability to get in some flying time. He tells the pilots he has a pilot's license though not as a rated Army aviator. The L-19's can be flown from the front or back seat so he badgers the pilots into letting him fly the aircraft from the back seat.

Powers, after a trip to Ban Me Thuot, returns saying he looked up the Major's medical records and a reason the Major is not rated is because he has vertigo.

Even when not flying with the Major, the pilots still spend time over our District looking for Viet Cong in the vast, tree covered, unpopulated wilderness extending west from Highway 14 to the Cambodian border.

On one reconnaissance to the west, Smith wipes out a herd of water buffaloes

82

Quiet Times

with his rockets. He brags on his next visit about all the Viet Cong water buffaloes killed. Unfortunately, the buffaloes belong to a Montagnard Buon on the Mewal trail. After the hamlet chief complains, Na Han asks us to tell the pilots not to shoot just because it moves.

Several weeks later, I fly to Ban Me Thuot with Smith. En route, he diverts from the normal flight path to fly over an abandoned village in An Loc District. The week before he had killed some Viet Cong there with his rockets. He wants to look for others.

We fly low over the ruins. Once this was a large hamlet with well-constructed cement buildings. Roofing sheet metal lays on the ground or hangs a few feet above it. After flying back and fourth, Smith, points down yelling that someone is hiding under some sheet metal. He dives at what he sees, pulling up a few feet from the ground.

I see nothing and nothing moves. Then making another pass he buzzes the same area. I aim my carbine out the back window. On the second pass, the sheet metal is thrown off and a black pajama clad figure jumps up and starts running; Smith laughs and yells at me to shoot. I see the target but tell him I am not going to shoot "mama san;" we fly on to Ban Me Thuot.

The Major wants to reward the pilots as an incentive for their continued help. The pilots have heard about nam-pay and ask that we take them to a Buon to try it.

Na Han is approached and makes arrangements for a visit to Buon Trieng.

There are two Buon Triengs, one Montagnard, the other Vietnamese. I have no idea why they have the same name other than they are next to each other.

The hamlet chief in the Montagnard Buon Trieng was recently elected and owes Na Han. The election was democracy at its finest. All candidates for chief lined up in the hamlet's center facing Na Han. The men in the hamlet lined up behind their choice. The winner was the one with the most men standing behind him.

The pilots' visit is arranged for Sunday afternoon. They are to drive out and

Our War

back from Ban Me Thuot the same day.

Sunday is a good day to travel. The Vietnamese are as serious about their weekend as they are about the daily three-hour siesta between 12 and 3. No work is done including, if it can be avoided, fighting. I worry that someday the Viet Cong will walk into the compound during siesta as often not even the gate guard is awake. Luckily the Viet Cong keep the same schedule.

That Sunday, after the pilots arrive, I take them to the Buon. The Major went to Ban Me Thuot for the weekend.

The hamlet chief meets us and we walk over to his long house. As we approach, an attractive Montagnard woman walks out on the long house deck next to the chief's and starts speaking to us in "pidgin" English saying she works for the Americans at Pleiku. Then a young, blond, light skinned boy about two, runs out. Taking one look at the fair skin men talking to his mother he starts screaming. His mother lifts him up, carrying him still screaming into her long house.

Entering his house, the chief brings out a nam-pay jug. The pilots enjoy it, quickly getting sloshed, not realizing how potent the odd tasting brew is. The chief enjoys himself. After finding out they are pilots he gives each a copper bracelet.

Then a bird flies into the long house—everyone is yelling and moving—if it flies out someone in the house will die. A pilot pulls his .45 to shoot; luckily the bird is caught before he fires; no one is going to die. The pilots make it safely back to Ban Me Thuot.

On most weekends nothing goes on. The District staff normally goes to Ban Me Thuot to see their families. We also go to Ban Me Thuot for Saturday night, rotating who gets to go.

On Saturday afternoon, about once a month, Stephanau invites the Major, Na Han, and me to his house for drinks and lunch. Normally this lasts until four or five in the afternoon. In return we bring Johnny Walker, which we buy cheap at the PX.

Lunch is excellent French cuisine served by Stephanau's young Vietnamese

Quiet Times

female cook. Crystals of chilled Portuguese rose that Stephanau imports by the barrel accompany the meal.

We talk about everything but the war. Stephanau wants to hunt a tiger killing buffalo in the District. His plan is to stake out a buffalo at night, with me posted in a blind up a tree. I treat it as a joke. Sitting on his verandah on a sunny Saturday afternoon, drinking scotch with ice, makes it easy to forget the war

Stephanau, a Corsican, has several partners in the plantation. His wife, who remains in France, is a member of the French family that originally built the plantation. The other partners are the other male family members. The partners take turns staying in Vietnam operating the plantation, the District's most important business.

The French Korean Battalion's journey to its destruction in Bernard Fall's book, *Street without Joy,* begins here at plantation Rossi. Now the Viet Cong leave the plantation and Stephanau alone. Their inactivity on the plantation fuels rumors about payoffs. Na Han also keeps his distance because it is hard to predict what the Saigon government may do against the remaining French. Na Han seldom goes to the plantation; I go whenever invited.

On Sunday, Stephanau travels to Ban Me Thuot to visit the other French plantation owners. One Sunday he invites the Major to go with him to play cards at a French plantation near Ban Me Thuot. The Major, wearing civilian clothes, goes in Stephanau's beat up Citroen.

After the Major leaves, Warrant Officer Duc comes into our office. We talk about the Montagnards. Eventually the conversation gets around to my desire to obtain a decent field knife. Duc tells me there is a Buon, near old Buon Ho, where I can get a good knife at a cheap price.

Bored, with nothing to do, leaving Stedman on the compound radio, Dian, Powers, Duc and I load into the jeep and drive the dirt road to old Buon Ho.

The jeep is rigged for cross-country travel: the canvas roof removed so that you

Our War

can get out rapidly, sandbags stacked on the floor to protect passengers from mine shrapnel, the windshield down giving a three hundred and sixty degree field of fire. The one thing missing is a welded upright bar on the front bumper extending the height of a seated passenger; its purpose to cut wires stretched across a road intended to decapitate jeep riders with windshields down.

Captain Yee, in charge at old Buon Ho, is awake and sober when we drive up. He argues against our going to Duc's Buon; it is about a kilometer walk beyond old Buon Ho. Viet Cong could be there. Finally, with three Popular Force soldiers, he comes along for security.

The Buon, when we get there, is the poorest, most decrepit I have been in. But the people want to do business. The hamlet chief takes us into his long house and we sit around drinking nam-pay, while haggling over trade goods. They have knives, pipes and crossbows, all low quality. I buy some, too embarrassed to leave with nothing after all the fuss.

No one feels any pain by the time we get back to the jeep.

Driving back, near Stephanau's, we pass a small lake with a tiny duck waddling around the middle.

Duc, standing up on the rear seat, yells at Powers who is driving to back up.

Powers backs the jeep, then stops. Duc fires his carbine at the duck, missing. Eight more shots miss.

Fifty yards away, the duck waddles contemptuously around the pond ignoring the shots splashing around it. Laughing, no one saying anything, we all jump up, put our carbines on automatic, emptying the magazines, demolishing the duck.

Duc, taking off his harness and leaving his carbine, jumps into the pond and wades out grabbing the carcass while we cheer him on.

Our mood is broken when we get back to the compound; the Major has returned early. Stedman meets us at the gate and says the Major is fuming because we left without his permission. All the Major says, however, is to let him know beforehand when

Quiet Times

we leave the compound.

The mines by the old District headquarters are removed.

A young cow herder runs into the minefield chasing some cattle and is blown up.

The mines, "bouncing betties," have a small wire that protrudes above the ground; stepping on the wire sets off the mine.

The Major asks Province to send engineers with mine sweeping equipment to clear the field. With the minefield centered in a populated area sooner or later someone else will wander in and get killed.

In the morning a week after the boy dies an ARVN Engineer Lieutenant drives into the compound in a truck carrying an engineer squad. Speaking fluent English, he is from Brooklyn, he tells me that they are to clear the minefield.

While talking with the Lieutenant, I glance into his truck and notice that there is no mine detector. In answer to my question as to his equipment he says he has none. He explains that one soldier has a sensitive toe. He will find the mines by walking barefoot through the brush locating the wires protruding above ground by feel.

Presumably they do, all day there are explosions down by the old District headquarters; the engineers are gone at the end of the day.

Dian and I, both Catholics, decide to attend Sunday Mass in the hamlets. There are two Catholic churches, one in Ha Lan the other in the Vietnamese Buon Trieng.

First we try Buon Trieng. The service is odd. The men sit on one side, the women on the other, and with the recent Vatican Council doing away with universal Latin use, the words are in Vietnamese.

No matter where you travel in the world the Mass is the same, but here it is strange.

Ha Lan the following Sunday is the same.

After the service, Dian makes a great show checking that the jeep is not

Our War

"booby" trapped. It was parked in the church courtyard during Mass. He crawls under it, lifts the hood, looks under the seats. I feel like a jerk.

After that I attend Mass with the Army chaplain in Ban Me Thuot.

Most time is spent honing our volleyball skills.

The artillery platoon Sergeant is a good player. Using the younger members on the District staff he trains a team that often beats us. The Americans, however, sometimes win; taller and more aggressive, we control the net. Most afternoons games are played in the open area by the headquarters building until dusk.

In the evening, after dinner, we play cards or listen to Stedman's Panasonic short wave radio, hoping to pick up the English language missionary stations in the Philippines playing American music.

A month after ordering the Special Services movie projector we receive its cinemascope lens. A due out card comes with it for the rest of the projector. Hopefully this means that the projector is not too far behind.

In the meantime, the United States Information Services (USIS) director at Ban Me Thuot agrees to lend us a projector until the Special Services projector shows up. The deal requires the team to show movies to the locals.

Y'Don willingly has his Popular Force soldiers build an outdoor movie theater inside the compound. The back of the police station is the screen. Log benches are built extending out to the bunker line for the audience.

Rather than show dull USIS propaganda, we obtain feature movies or TV reruns from Army Special Services. Though the movies are in English, there is always a crowd. The Rhade like westerns and viewing the TV series *Combat*, about a World War II American infantry squad fighting the Germans. They reveal their bias, cheering the Indians in the westerns, and the Germans in *Combat*.

Special Services carries the latest stateside movies. We get any we want.

Quiet Times

During the war the only movie impossible to get is the GI's favorite, Jane Fonda's *Barbarella*. It is always signed out.

Special Services also puts out a daily newspaper, *The Star and Stripes*.

Nothing controversial is in it but each issue contains casualty lists and their units. Reading these tells where the battles are and how we are doing.

The 101st takes heavy casualties at Dak To in Kontum. A former West Point football player makes headlines calling in napalm on his company.

Captain Vurlumis makes the casualty list, killed in action.

Two Popular Force soldiers are shot to death near the duck massacre site on Sunday afternoon two weeks after our buying trip to old Buon Ho.

Our War

Stephenau, Rossi plantation partner—celebrating Tet

VC Are Here!

CHAPTER SIX

American combat units move into the highlands during the planting season. Convoys move overland from Nah Trang to Highway 14 and then roll north to Pleiku or further north to Kontum Province. The team is happy seeing these convoys. The road to Ban Me Thuot is cleared with Regional and Popular Force sweeping the entire length. We can use it with little risk.

The first American unit is an Engineer Construction Company. The evening before it arrives, Province orders that the District Popular Force sweep and secure the Ha Lan pass. I drive up in the morning to check that it is open. Our PF are at the top relaxing, some sleeping, others sitting around boiling tea.

The Engineer Company arrives at dusk. Standing on a District compound bunker Na Han and I watch as the column headlights move up Highway 14. As they reach the compound turnoff he turns and says tell the "French" to go into camp at the hill's base. We looked at each other; Na Han then laughs saying "I mean the Americans."

Driving down to the Company Commander, I tell him where to camp. He does by circling the trucks.

In the morning Na Han and I walk to the camp. The five-ton dump trucks are loaded with metal desks, chairs, filing cabinets and typewriters. It strikes me as an odd way to fight a war.

On seeing us the Company Commander complains that he received sniper fire all night. Na Han smiles and tells the Captain that it was not snipers, just hunters hunting by flashlight in the night. The Captain is skeptical. I do not bother telling him that almost every man in the District has a rifle.

Around 1000 hours a Mechanized Company from the 25th Division at Pleiku arrives. The Engineers then head north with the escort.

Though the Vietnamese and American military need armed convoys to use the highway, the Vietnamese civilians use it at will. Cargo trucks, buses, autos and Lambrettas move freely between the various hamlets and the larger cities.

Our War

The war is profitable for many people. New Mercedes Benz tractor-trailer trucks travel daily between Pleiku and Ban Me Thuot. The Viet Cong control points on the highways extract taxes—with a receipt given—but seldom attack anyone.

The highway is not used at night. It is both dangerous and inconvenient. At dusk the hamlets on the highway lock their gates. Moving then on the highway requires unlikely success in approaching the armed gate guards and convincing them to open to strangers and their vehicle.

There are also private entrepreneurs who set up their own roadblocks on the District's fringes. The highwaymen caught are local Popular Force soldiers using their government-supplied weapons.

The District jail, the bunker in the compound's center, holds the Popular Force soldiers who try this added income source. No trial is held. They are kept there a few weeks with their family feeding them, then released.

Though difficult to tell if violence is by bandits or the Viet Cong, everyone gives the Viet Cong full credit.

Viet Cong tax collection puts Stephanau in a bad situation.

One Friday evening, after returning with frozen shrimp from the Mess Sergeant in Ban Me Thuot, I drive to Stephanau's. I want to exchange some shrimp for horseradish, tabasco and ketchup to make a sauce.

Stephanau's smoke filled living room is crowded with Chinese playing cards. He tells me his problem. He cannot ship his coffee and tea to the markets in Saigon without payoffs to the Viet Cong. But he fears that if bribes are given Saigon will confiscate the plantation and deport him.

He explains that these Chinese are from Cholon to buy his crop.

They will ship and pay off the Viet Cong. They will also pay him outside the country, evading the currency laws. That way he can get his money to France. But he complains he makes a lot less using these middlemen.

VC Are Here!

Though our team always travels armed in our own vehicles, the Vietnamese military, particularly the junior officers and enlisted men, have no access to government vehicles.

When traveling on leave to see their families they wear civilian clothes and use local transportation—buses, trucks or Lambrettas. Papers identifying them as Army Republic of Vietnam soldiers are not carried. They fear assassination if stopped.

One day while riding back in our jeep from Ban Me Thuot a bus going towards the city passes. The vehicles fly by each other at seventy miles an hour. In those few seconds the bus driver smiles and waves; he looks like Lieutenant Long.

Several days later I mention to Long that I saw a bus driver that looks like him.

Long answers by saying that he intends to survive this war. His parents need him. Pulling out his wallet he shows me his parents and a brother's picture. Originally he had a large family but now he and his brother, an ARVN Ranger Sergeant at Pleiku, survive. His parents live in Saigon and were Viet Minh. The French killed his other brothers.

Then giving me his lopsided smile, he says that he always drives the bus. The Viet Cong will never suspect that the driver is an officer.

The Major remains obsessed about his mail. Though our airstrip is now approved with L-19's landing frequently, he continues to badger the enlisted men to drive to Ban Me Thuot. He wants them to go daily; saying the road is safe. There has never been an ambush on it.

Dian and Bozilov are reluctant. The Major expends more and more energy cajoling, intimidating and threatening before they will make the trip. Gradually, over time, he becomes incensed at them. His anger is primarily focused at Dian. He never forgets that Dian went over his head and complained to Sector about Bearfoot's woman. Further, Dian continues to be critical of the Major's failure to push for operations. Dian

Our War

makes sure Sector knows his views.

Finally one evening over tea and cards, the Major explodes at Dian.

The previous night Dian and Powers had stayed in Ban Me Thuot. Dian has a shiner on his right eye when they return. He says nothing. Powers tells us that they had been in the NCO club the prior evening when a Sergeant called Dian a faggot. They fought and the NCO "beat the shit" out of Dian. The Major, aware of this when we sit down to play, starts ragging Dian.

"Sergeant Dian, are you sure you can see the cards tonight?"

"Yeah," he responds as the cards are dealt.

"You know it looks like you have some dirt around your eye."

We continue play, no one saying anything other than making their bids. Dian makes a run and the Major eats the queen of spades.

"Sergeant Dian, I hear someone been talking about you at the NCO club."

Dian, winning the card game, looks up responding, "Yea, they talk about you too."

"What do you mean?"

"They say you keep telling them we're having contacts when everyone knows we're sitting on our asses."

The Major pauses, his face turns red, and then he jumps up from the table and orders me to walk with him around the compound.

Walking the compound perimeter, he vents his anger, pounding his fists. I say nothing.

He talks about Pusan and the guts it took to stand and fight there. Though it is a cool evening, he is sweating profusely; taking off his fatigue blouse, he threatens to fight Dian then and there. Eventually after walking around and around the compound, he calms down.

I remind him Dian has asked for a transfer to a line unit; he agrees to transfer Dian as soon as a replacement is available.

VC Are Here!

That is the last nightly card game.

A week later the ARVN battalion with my advisor buddy from Germany comes up the highway. The battalion is after the local Viet Cong Battalion 301. The intelligence summary from Province constantly reports the unit sighted in the District. To me the reports lack credibility. Our Montagnard spies, who still periodically show up to collect a little extra money, never mention 301.

The ARVN battalion, traveling in trucks, pulls off the highway to our north, dismounts, and moves overland to the northeast.

That night it bivouacs outside radio range from everyone but the District. Our team talks to the battalion advisor using the PRC-25 radio.

I establish a radio watch in the bunker. Whoever we have on the radio can talk to the battalion advisor and using the AM radio in the bunker relay to Sector, which has a twenty-four hour radio watch. Powers and Stedman volunteer to take shifts during the night.

During the day I explain the arrangements to the Major because he is sleeping in the bunker.

After Regiment 18B passed, we all started sleeping in the "Co-loc-bo." We also moved the stove, refrigerator and kitchen table there. That way when cooking Bo would have no reason to come into the office.

Vietnamese Sergeants from the District staff still share the "Co-loc-bo" with us. There part is separated from us by a bamboo partition. In the evenings, the Vietnamese Sergeants jabber and talk until the early morning.

The Major wants the whole building. He wants the Sergeants evicted. He tells Na Han he cannot sleep in the "Co-loc-bo" with the noise. Na Han refuses to kick the Sergeants out. The Major decides to sleep in the communication bunker until he can get the Sergeants kicked out.

This evening, the Major coming into the bunker to sleep seems surprised to see

Our War

Powers, Stedman, Dian and myself listening to the radio traffic. Turning to Stedman who is on the radio he orders "Turn the radio off, I'm going to sleep."

I answer "Sir, the radios have to stay on, it's the only contact the battalion has with Ban Me Thuot if something happens."

"Nothing 's going to happen; turn the radios off so I can get to sleep."

"Sir, we told them we'd monitor the net, if something happens there's no way they can reach Ban Me Thuot; we've got to keep the radios on all night."

"Turn the radios off."

"Sir, they have to be manned all night."

"Well I'm not going to man them."

"Sir," interjects Dian, "Stedman and Powers have volunteered."

Everyone is now looking at the Major. Even in the bunker's dim light he can be seen turning bright red. Without saying anything, he stomps to his bed, grabs his bedding and leaves, saying as he walks up the steps that "I'll sleep in Bearfoot's old bunker."

Stedman and Powers take turns on the radio, fighting the rats that are surprised to find anyone up.

Nothing happens.

The battalion advisor calls us at six the next morning; the battalion is moving.

Immediately he is back up, "Alpha, this is four-four, I hear shots, I'm moving there," a short pause, then, "some of my men are laying on the ground, over."

Shortly he calmly reports, "Alpha, we've walked into an ambush, they're shooting from all around us, I've got dead and wounded, over."

Stedman calls An Loc District to our south. They raise Ban Me Thuot.

In the interim, our two howitzers begin firing. Within minutes an Air Force Forward Air Controller (FAC) is overhead in his "Bird-dog." The artillery fire ceases while air strikes are brought in. The Viet Cong ambush collapses.

The Major never mentions the previous evening's conversation.

VC Are Here!

The attack dismays me. The Viet Cong moved a main force battalion within our artillery fan yet our local spies reported nothing. With a lot less effort they can set an ambush on the highway. I tell the Major I am not using the highway unless I have to.

The Sergeants, under protest, continue to go. They are upset, knowing that they are needlessly putting their lives on the line.

Things finally boil over.

After not receiving mail from Sector via the "Bird-dog" for a few days, the Major tells the Sergeants to drive in and get his mail, even though we are well supplied with everything—beer, drinking water, food and gas.

Dian and Bozilov try to sweet talk the Major by arguing that there is no need to go, he can wait for the next plane. The Major starts huffing, begins turning red, complaining that the pilots are too unreliable and besides the road is safe.

Finally both Sergeants tell the Major that there is no reason to go to Ban Me Thuot and they are not going. The Major's face becomes bright red, as he rants that they are cowards, then turning he walks off, yelling he will go himself. Then getting some Popular Force soldiers, he loads them in the jeep and drives off to Ban Me Thuot.

As the Major drives out the gate, the two Sergeants standing silently at the office door watching him leave rush over to the "Co-loc-bo" and grab their weapons. Anger is in their faces.

I catch up with them in the compound courtyard as they head for the gate, asking, "Where are you going?"

Bozilov, stone faced, answers "We're going to "Howard Johnson's" to get some people to ambush the jeep in the pass when it comes back."

I tell them to go back to the office and sit down. We have a couple of beers; they cool off.

The Sergeants are concerned that the Major's obsession with his own problems will get us all killed.

Our War

Also the Major has talked about bugging out ever since told we would be abandoned if hit. No one agrees with this.

I tell them I will talk to Sector about getting him or us transferred.

I feel like a character in The *Caine* Mutiny.

The one thing not done In the American military is going over your boss's head. However, after the radio incident and the problems with the Sergeants, I realize that the situation with the Major is getting beyond my control. If something happens, I want to insure everyone is involved including the Sector advisor, a rear guard action to cover my ass.

On my next trip to Ban Me Thuot I tell the company grade advisors whose quarters I share about the radio incident. They urge me to see the Sector advisor, Lieutenant Colonel Monroe. I refuse telling them I do not want to talk about problems with the Major. Finally, like Baer Rabbit in the brier patch, Lieutenant Colonel Monroe, spurred by his Captains, orders me to tell him what is going on in the District.

The Captains have their own personal vendetta against the Major. The Major infuriates Sector by telling anyone who listens that the staff there are cowards afraid to ride the highway to visit us. Upset at the Major's constant criticism, they are particularly angered after his recent complaint to the division senior advisor.

The division senior advisor, the baldhead at Ban Me Thuot, got a plum assignment as a brigade commander with the 1st Cav. Prior to his transfer, he visited each District, ours for the first and only time.

For some reason he brought the Advisor team doctor along. A big mistake as the doctor was upset. The Colonel had ordered the doctor to sign a certificate that the Colonel had a wound from enemy contact so he could get a Purple Heart. The doctor sarcastically calls the Colonel a hero, saying that the injury was from sitting on a "punji" stake.

The Colonel's time as an advisor to the Vietnamese was not wasted; he learnt well. His visit is designed to get a parting gift from each District chief.

He wants a six shooter from Na Han. Na Han gives him one still in its original packing.

The Major, with all this good will available, complains to the Colonel that the team is in dire straits, unsupported by Sector. If Sector ships some gravel and sand then we could fix up the "Co-loc-bo," by laying a concrete floor.

The Colonel, returning to Ban Me Thuot, tells Monroe to get the gravel and sand.

Not surprisingly Monroe and the assistant Province advisor Bonds are thus predisposed to listen as I tell my story. They say they have heard the same from other sources, but think I am overly dramatic. They promise to transfer Dian because the Major wants him out. Everyone else stays; the Major rotates home soon.

For the next few weeks I travel, first to Saigon for more schooling on the hamlet evaluation report, then to Mewal to spend a week working with the Regional Force company stationed there.

A month after my meeting with Monroe, the Major receives orders to escort a rock and roll band around Vietnam for Special Services. The Major sputters and eventually gets it changed.

Our War

SFC Bozilov (L), SFC Dian (Standing), Sp-5 Powers

The Rice War Begins

CHAPTER SEVEN

The monsoons, heavy rains that come during the highland's planting season, begin each day about four in the afternoon and last one or two hours.

The steady downpours limit visibility and turn roads and trails other than a hardtop into muddy quagmires.

The monsoon season varies depending on your location in Vietnam. Correspondents in Saigon lose credibility after reporting monsoons effecting combat operations in the highlands based on Saigon's weather.

The rice harvest begins with the ending of the monsoons. Like the Scot galloglasses who came to Ireland for the fighting season after the harvest in Scotland, the Viet Cong will begin their attacks after the harvest.

Con Diem, a large Vietnamese hamlet outside the artillery fan, is the main rice grower for the District's Viet Cong.

Na Han walks into our office and says he has decided to run an operation against it.

The attack is a major operation. Na Han needs both Province approval and additional Regional Force and Truong Son companies. To provide artillery support the howitzers will have to move to old Buon Ho and remain there overnight. Province will not let that happen unless the howitzers are guarded by at least one Regional Force company.

A plan is developed. The Major flies north to the Special Forces camp. They agree to move overland and hit the village while District forces will move at night into blocking positions.

Province loans Na Han two additional Regional Force companies.

The CIA reluctantly contributes another Truong Son company after much pleading on my part during a visit to their Ban Me Thuot residence. The CIA advisors make clear that this is the last time we can use the Truong Son in a military operation.

101

Our War

On the first day of the operation the two 105-MM howitzers move at dusk to the open field outside old Buon Ho. Con Diem is now within the artillery fan.

The District compound's Regional Force company and four Popular Force platoons take up positions around the open field to provide security for the guns. Popular Force units from the Catholic villages of Ha Lan and Buon Trieng are brought into the District compound to secure it for the night.

After dark, the two Regional Force companies from Province move in one column while the two Truong Son companies, one from Province and our local one, in another. It is seven kilometers cross country to the blocking positions.

Moving at night cross-country is always tough. This night is exhausting; there is no moon and little starlight. Distances are hard to judge; you see nothing but dark shapes moving to your front.

As the night progresses the mind wanders. You walk oblivious for long periods until the column jerks to a stop and you are jogged wide-awake by hitting the man in front. A distance that takes less than three hours to walk in daylight requires twice that time. Often like an accordion the column jerks to a stop and then runs to catch up as the guide finds a familiar path and picks up the pace.

My column's movement is uneventful.

The other column kills its point man.

When switching points, the point man steps off the trail to allow the new point to take his place. As he steps back onto the trail, someone following shoots him through the head thinking he is a Viet Cong.

This is the second killing like this in four months. A Popular Force soldier returning from a night ambush outside Quan Lie was killed when he stepped off the trail to piss. Na Han later told me the shooter had not made a mistake. The dead man's wife was the shooter's girl friend.

The blocking positions are reached before dawn. At first light, the Special Forces attack.

The Rice War Begins

After a quick fight, the Viet Cong abandon the village fleeing between the blocking positions into the swamp at the village's end and are gone.

The swamp was on the map used in planning the operation. When the Major and I sat with Na Han in his office drafting the plan I argued that the blocking positions were too far away. The Viet Cong could retreat into the swamp. Na Han dismissed this saying there was no need to block the swamp, it was too much of an obstacle. For some reason, the Major, who from his military experience knew a swamp is not an obstacle to infantry, agreed with Na Han, overruling me.

Except for two Viet Cong village guards killed by the Special Forces and a wounded man without weapon who wanders into our position, the Viet Cong escape.

The Sergeant leading the Special Forces unit is furious at our failure to block the Viet Cong escape. He tells the Major he will never work with the District again.

Three days later while the team is eating supper in the "Co-loc-bo," the compound erupts with yelling. Thinking we are under attack, grabbing our rifles, we rush outside to find Na Han and everyone else in the compound running back and forth, screaming hysterically.

A small deer is struggling in the barbed wire. Everyone is waving his or her arms, trying to drive it back the way it came. Finally the frightened deer jumps the last wire into the compound, then bounds across the compound and out over the barbed wire on the other side.

Na Han, still sweating from his exertion, walks over to us. For the first time since I have known him he looks terrified.

His composure lost, his faced drained of color, looking wide-eyed at me, in a shaking voice he states, "The compound is going to be wiped out. When a deer goes through the wire, the compound is going to be wiped out. It happened before."

Na Han is gone within three weeks.

Our War

The new District chief is Captain Yen. A Rhade, former 23rd Division recon company commander, French Legion of Honor recipient, veteran of numerous battles under the French and Vietnamese banner, a Christian recently converted by the Evangelists in Ban Me Thuot; he is a reformed alcoholic returning to his home District.

He goes native within a week after his return.

When you need him, if not in his office, check and see if there is a funeral. Like the Irish, the Montagnards send their dead off with a "grand" party. Yen will be there drinking nam-pay. He and Captain Yee are best buddies. Yee now leads every combat operation.

Reports of FULRO activity also increase.

Na Han kept the FULRO movement underground. The Viet Cong were simply a nuisance put up with compared to Na Han's virulent hatred of FULRO. One night Na Han fired artillery blind all night hoping to kill FULRO based on a rumor that a FULRO column was moving along the trail from old Dat Hieu to Mewal. He never wasted that much artillery on the Viet Cong.

Yen, however, is a secret or perhaps not so secret FULRO supporter. He brags to me that his nephews are with FULRO.

Yen permits a Special Forces recruiting team to operate in the District. During the week the team has an American Special Forces NCO with it. Besides the American Sergeant the team has two Montagnard CIDG Sergeants, and two very attractive, quite frankly extremely beautiful, young Montagnard women.

On weekends the American NCO, like most of the Vietnamese District staff, returns to Ban Me Thuot. With the American gone, the recruiting team uses the Special Forces 2 1/2-ton truck to go to the Buons recruiting for FULRO.

Lieutenant Long tells me that the ranking Montagnard Sergeant in the recruiting team is the District FULRO chief while the two women, dressed in tiger fatigues and armed with Thompson submachine guns, are his bodyguards.

The Rice War Begins

I soon find out that their beauty does not lessen their female tendency towards genocide.

The Vietnamese staff at the District is upset at Yen's failure to stop the FULRO recruiting.

One Saturday, the Vietnamese Intelligence NCO, Sergeant Thuong, takes it upon himself to resolve the problem. While the FULRO chief is having an espresso at "Howard Johnson's," Thuong takes a shot at him with his .45. Luckily for the FULRO chief, Thuong shoots as accurately as our stateside Mafioso. He is only wounded.

That night the elderly civilian chief administrator of the District throws a party at his home in Buon Trieng to celebrate twenty-five years in office. Stephanau, his Vietnamese plantation manager, myself, and most of the ranking Montagnards are there including Yee and Yen.

The party is in a small ground level bamboo building that looks like it was built as a barn for water buffaloes and cows. This impression is reinforced by large straw bales stacked along the rear wall covered with a tarpaulin that is used as a seat after several hours drinking nam-pay, rice wine and whiskey.

Long after dark, the FULRO chief and his two female bodyguards walk into the party.

The room becomes silent; the FULRO chief is not invited. The administrative chief, however, makes him feel welcome, quickly showing why he has successfully stayed in office for twenty-five years through numerous government changes.

I find out for the first time that the FULRO chief is shot. He shows everyone his bandaged arm in a sling. He talks about the ambush, telling anyone who cares that it is a slight wound.

To relieve the tension, Stephanau takes some pictures; all continue to drink, talking, enjoying themselves.

Then one of the women bodyguards notices the Vietnamese foreman. Pointing

Our War

her Thompson submachine gun at him, she starts to yell. The poor man cowers. All start talking and raising their voices at once. In the midst of the rising crescendo Stephanau tells me that the women want to kill the foreman because he is Vietnamese.

The Thompson's in the girls' hands and a pistol in the FULRO chiefs are the only weapons visible. I assume others have concealed weapons.

Stuck in the belt hidden under my recently obtained jungle fatigue blouse is a .45.

No one is paying attention to me sitting on the thatch pile, my back against the bamboo wall. The women and FULRO chief are sitting to my side. The Vietnamese foreman, Stephanau and the administrative chief are standing to our front arguing with them.

I slide the pistol to my front, releasing the safety. I will shoot the women if they make a move to shoot the foreman. There is no doubt in my mind that they will kill Stephanau and me if they kill the foreman.

But good sense prevails; Stephanau convinces them that the foreman will not talk to the Vietnamese authorities about this meeting between the FULRO and District chief. The party resumes.

Stephanau takes more photos, posing the girls around me cradling their Thompson's. The picture taking session satiates their desire to kill.

Next time I have lunch at the plantation, Stephanau gives me the picture as a memento.

Yen uses his assignment as chief in his home District to enrich his family.

The old District headquarters sitting at the road junction between Highway 14 and old Buon Ho is a valuable business property now that the landmines are gone. Yen, like most Rhade men, has several ex-wives. Montagnard society is matriarchal; women own everything and serial polygamy is the norm. Shortly after his arrival one ex-wife builds a wooden building at the crossroads and opens a successful restaurant.

While Yen cares for his family he refuses to take charge as District chief. No

The Rice War Begins

decisions are made, papers signed, projects initiated or supervised. He either sits aloof in his office refusing to see anyone or goes to a Montagnard Buon for nam-pay. He dislikes his Vietnamese staff, and ignores his Regional Force company commander and artillery platoon leader.

Na Han made decisions and as advisors we advised, if asked. With Yen a vacuum exists. Gradually the advisory team fills the void by making Yen's decisions. His staff is willing to do what we ask since they can blame us if something goes wrong.

The team gets involved in the nitty-gritty, determining where the new cement wells go, who gets the goods from USAID, when and where to run operations, training, staffing and supplying the hamlet medics; we have our nose into most everything.

I do the talking with Yen. The Major refuses to speak to him since Yen is an alcoholic. Instead the Major spends his time drinking coffee in the "Co-loc-bo" with the pilots or running back and forth to Ban Me Thuot to get his mail.

Yen tells me one day while sipping cafe-au-lait in his ex-wife's new restaurant that he never wanted to be District chief in his home District. No matter what he does someone is mad. In the end it will hurt his family.

He wants to go back to the division and his old job as the recon company commander. But now, he adds, he helps his family as best he can as he sweeps his arm around the restaurant telling me it belongs to an ex-wife. Then pointing at his chest, he jokes, "Je suis le conseiller, vous etes le chef du District," he is the advisor, the Americans are the District chief.

A month into Yen's tour as chief, Province sends Captain Hoy to assist him. Hoy, a Montagnard refugee from North Vietnam, has ingratiated himself with the Vietnamese, taking a Vietnamese name. Rumor is that Hoy, titled director of operations, will replace Yen when the politics permit. Right now Yen cannot be replaced since the division commander is Yen's friend.

At first Hoy's appointment creates problems for us. With Yen we had our way.

Our War

Yen's little joke that the advisors run the District is not too off. Hoy is sent to keep the Americans under control; everything is to go through him. Unlike Yen, he wants to run the District so he keeps his distance from the Americans. But his weakness is soon discovered. A Pall Mall chain smoker, he relaxes with us when we start bringing him cartons from the PX.

Language Problems

CHAPTER EIGHT

Dong, our last interpreter, had been sleeping in the "Co-loc-bo." After Yen arrives, the Major succeeds in having the Vietnamese Sergeants evicted. Dong, angry with us for taking his sleeping area, goes AWOL, never to return.

Without a translator, Nguyen long gone, it is difficult to talk with, let alone advise the Vietnamese. What I remember of my high school and college French helps me carry on conversations, though limited to the present tense. Most Vietnamese officers speak French; unfortunately, lots better than I do. They rather speak and practice their English.

Language problems can lead to misunderstandings. Lieutenant Long continually tells me that he is going to jail when he goes to Ban Me Thuot. He makes these trips about twice a month, a lot of jail time.

Eventually, we clear it up. In the past some American jokingly told Long that when Long went to see his wife he was going to jail; Long did not get the joke.

We all know a little Vietnamese but Stedman, who spends hours studying the language and teaching the Vietnamese English, develops proficiency. When needed he works as our interpreter.

On the other hand reading a Vietnamese operations order is not difficult. Key information is graphic using American military symbols and I have picked up a smattering of Vietnamese military terms. Operation orders are primarily graphic overlays placed on a map and through symbols tell what each unit is to do and when.

Vietnamese is easy to read. The French translated the Vietnamese language into the Greco-Roman alphabet so that unlike other oriental languages - such as Thai, Chinese or Japanese, with their own alphabets - written Vietnamese is easy for the Western eye to comprehend.

On operations, Yee and I speak French. I can convey what I want done with gestures and my limited Vietnamese and French, but I am dependent on the Vietnamese who speak English to tell me what is going on.

Our War

A new Regional Force company replaces the one Warrant Officer Duc was assigned. The company commander from Saigon speaks no French but does speak English, though poorly.

The natural field leader in the company is a tall Montagnard Platoon Sergeant who everyone refers to as the 'Chef de Platoon." In the field he runs the company, all the Sergeants deferring to him. This company seems better trained then Duc's. At least on operations it throws out flank and point security.

With Yen as District chief, our walks to the outlying Buons become almost a daily routine.

Captain Yee is now nominally the operation commander. But the Regional Force company commander has to agree—a balance of power. Normally, I get to cast the deciding vote and if it really gets heated or I do not know what they are arguing about, I call District on the radio and the District chief makes the decision.

The language barrier, however, often leaves me in the dark as to what really is happening.

For example, when I first arrived in the District, Dat Hieu had a demonstration when the Buddhist riots were occurring in Hue. The local Boy Scout troop dressed in their uniforms set up a sympathy blockade on Highway 14 stopping traffic.

It is over before it really starts.

At that time Na Han told me that he told the Buddhists that, "If they want to demonstrate they should go to Ban Me Thuot. There is no sense rioting in Dat Hieu as no correspondents are going to report it."

That is Na Han's explanation. I think he told them to lift the blockade or he would shoot. The rioters were Vietnamese, not Montagnards. Na Han would shoot them without too much thought.

While the language differences are a minor problem in dealing with the military, it significantly hampers our work with the peasants in distributing the USAID

Language Problems

goods.

A major USAID project is to put cement wells into all the hamlets. Most of the hamlets draw water from nearby heavily polluted streams shared by pigs, cows, water buffaloes, dogs and people. Typhoid and cholera epidemics plague the hamlets.

In Buon Trieng over 40 people die within a few weeks including the Hamlet chief (which is why a new one was elected.) Powers working with the people there feels useless. They will not boil their water or draw it from another source.

A MEDCAP team inspects the hamlet and reconfirms that the hamlet needs a better water source. The hope is that water from wells deep in the earth will have less contamination. But after the wells are built, the Montagnards refuse to use them. For some reason, whether religious, aesthetic or custom, they continue to use the streams.

I talked Na Han into assembling the villagers. He told them that they should use the wells. They all smile, agree and continue to get their water from the stream. They continue to die until eventually the disease runs its course.

The language problem exposes us to serious disease.

Powers works every day in the vacant District hospital, a large multi-wing cement building built by USAID. There is no doctor. The District medical personnel, two midwives and a health worker trained in first aid, may or may not be there.

Powers and Stedman go to the hospital and handle sick call each weekday. Stedman provides security and acts as a translator. Both spend most days there. The patients form long lines in the hallway. Powers, assisted by the health worker, sees each in turn in a small room, the one room used in the hospital. He gives advice on sanitation, cleans wounds and pumps vitamins and antibiotics USAID provides into the sick.

Sometimes American Army doctors come out to the hospital or visit the hamlets as a MEDCAP team.

These young doctors are trained to work in the large stateside medical factories equipped with the latest medical machinery. Drafted into the Army after medical school

Our War

they lack practical healing arts. The myriad diseases, poor sanitation, and what they consider superstition overwhelm them.

Powers, a corpsman, accomplishes more, dealing with medical problems in practical terms and the people in human terms. Powers at least knows he is doing good.

At night the hospital wards are empty. There is no one to care for the sick.

Extremely ill patients are sent to the hospital in Ban Me Thuot or go home if they decide they will die. Patients know it is futile to go to Ban Me Thuot if cursed. Powers finds it hard to believe that a healthy man can die from a curse but accepts it after several do.

Several months after he starts at the hospital, I notice Powers is not taking his daily malaria pills.

These are two evil tasting black pills, one large, one small.

An Army Regulation mandates you take the pills daily. Not taking the pills is a court-martial offense. More important, not taking them exposes you to a deadly illness. If you come down with malaria the Army gives you a double whammy, you are both sick and given an Article 15. The presumption is you caught malaria because you did not take the pills.

Powers tells me there is no reason to take the pills. There has never been a case of malaria at the hospital. Any reason not to take them is welcomed. We all stop.

A few weeks later, Stephanau comes into the compound and asks to borrow some malaria tablets until he can get into Ban Me Thuot. Delighted finally that I know one thing about the District that he does not, I smugly inform him that there is no need for the tablets.

"Powers has never seen a case of malaria in the hospital."

Stephanau laughs.

"That is true," he says. "The malaria strain in the District is so deadly everyone dies before they get to the hospital."

Language Problems

We start taking the pills immediately.

LT. Long (l), PFC Stedman, and two members of the District intelligence staff

The Fight For Rice Continues

CHAPTER NINE

The rice harvest begins. Operations increase as both sides attempt to control the crop.

The Viet Cong, like all soldiers, "Travel on their stomach." If they get hungry enough, hopefully, they'll come in as "Chieu-Hoi."

Con Diem is the one remaining Vietnamese village in the District growing rice outside the artillery fan. Province decides to relocate the peasants to deny the Viet Cong this rice.

Before the rice is harvested, an ARVN battalion moves on the village, rounds up the inhabitants, loads them and their movable possessions in 2 1/2-ton trucks, and transports them to an open field near District. The villagers leave behind their National Liberation Front flags, festooned all over the hamlet including the local schoolhouse, as well as anything not movable.

Province officials lay out a site for their new hamlet at District. Those moved are issued blankets, rice and bulgur, cooking oil and surplus American military World War II OD "Ike" jackets with ROTC insignia, These become the latest fashion statement.

The new area given the Con Diem villagers is squeezed between the already existing hamlets located at the base of the District compound hill.

The move takes several days.

Everything not moved is torched.

The villagers lose both what ARVN steals as well as this years rice crop.

The first day I notice that the 2 1/2-ton trucks leave the villagers off at their new site but do not unload their pigs. The pigs continue down Highway 14 to Ban Me Thuot.

The American Captain advising the battalion tells me that the ARVN Battalion commander is doing the villagers a favor. He is buying all their pigs (at about a tenth of what they could get for them in Ban Me Thuot) because there is no space to raise them in their new hamlet. He refuses to tell the battalion commander to stop stealing.

I call Sector on the radio, complain about the stealing, and manage to save a few pigs.

When the rice around Con Diem is ready to harvest, Yen lets the villagers go daily to harvest it.

Reports soon reach him that the villagers are sharing the harvest with the Viet Cong. He refuses the villagers permission to harvest the remaining rice.

"Bird-dogs" flying over the fields report that the rice continues to be harvested although no one is seen in the fields.

Yen decides to go after the harvested rice and destroy it.

The Major, due to rotate, goes on this operation though he has gone on no other. Yen will personally lead the operation and the Major tells me he should be with the District chief.

The plan is to move in the morning with the artillery to old Buon Ho. The troops will then walk overland to Con Diem, destroy the rice, returning to the District compound the same day.

For once everything goes as planned. The artillery moves early in the morning to old Buon Ho; the infantry column moves out and rapidly covers the distance to the old Con Diem ruins.

Surprisingly, the Viet Cong have cached rather than moved the rice. Rice cradles, large wooden bins about 4 by 10 feet, with a 4 foot depth are found buried in the woods or under the burnt buildings.

I am with the guns. The Major radios for me to go back to Buon Ho and get a "Bird-dog" from Ban Me Thuot and fly over the target area.

Early that afternoon Smith flies in and we take off.

From the air we easily spot the trails worn in the high grass leading to the hidden caches. Flying over the hamlet I direct the column to the likely areas hiding rice.

The Fight For Rice Continues

With our ability to see trails from the air the column soon burns over twenty of these caches. Each holds a few tons.

Though there is no contact; the operation is a big success.

The Major on his return is exhilarated. The rice discovered was more then we thought there. The Major further exaggerates in his report to Province stating that we destroyed over a hundred tons.

For a few days the Major basks in his success, then the operation gradually fades from memory as our day to day activities continue.

Suddenly, from Province, all hell breaks loose. The report went up the chain of command as a brilliant success until it reaches Corps. There some bright staff officer asks why this fantastic haul of rice was destroyed. Corps staff jumps on Division, Division chews out Province, "shit flows down hill" to the District. Why, they now all ask, were trucks not used to evacuate the rice?

The Major drastically revises downward his figures as to rice destroyed. That seems to satisfy everyone.

A few days after the Con Diem operation, Yen excitedly comes to our office and says that a new "Chieu-Hoi" may interest us. Yen's excitement surprises me; he never shows emotion.

The "Chieu-Hoi" is a thin Vietnamese wearing a khaki uniform.

He explains that he is a recon officer from the 33rd North Vietnamese Army Regiment, a liberation regiment organized into three 400 man lightly armed battalions. Its mission is to attack hamlets where Saigon is attempting pacification.

The recon officer is in the District to find a base area for the regiment. The regiment is due in February.

The "Chieu-Hoi" is sent to Ban Me Thuot and soon forgotten.

The first American general officer, the Deputy MACV Commanding General on an inspection tour, visit the District right before the Major's departure. The Major

Our War

briefs him and they tour the compound.

The one question the general asks is about Regiment 18B. He says Saigon has no idea where it crossed the border into Vietnam before it reached the coastal plain. The Major tells the general he never heard of Regiment 18B.

Then the Major, never one to ignore an opportunity, shows the general how we are using self-help to overcome our lousy living conditions. Reminding the general that each MACV team is suppose to have its own building and generators, The Major takes the general to the "Co-loc-bo." There he has the NCOs and our one Private laying a cement floor and nailing up wood interior walls made from ammo boxes.

Stedman worked in construction laying cement before drafted and provides the expertise.

Sector sent two dump trucks with gravel and sand after the Division Senior Advisor's visit. The missionaries replaced the cement we gave them, abiding by their agreement.

The Major tells the general that though he obtained the material for the floor, he still needs other supplies and the 100 KW generators. The general nods and says he'll see what he can do.

The general and his entourage get in their helicopters and fly off.

The Major is jubilant; Province will do something about our living conditions now.

He is right!

That night the Sector Deputy Senior Advisor Bonds calls on the radio, "Why were the Sergeants doing manual labor when the general was there?"

Bonds orders us to complete the living quarters before doing anything else; it is our priority.

This is the Major's last good deed. He flies out a few days later, two days before the Tet holidays. His replacement has yet to arrive.

118

The Fight For Rice Continues

Stedman and Powers leave with him, they are going to Hawaii on R&R. There should be no problem with them and the Major gone as the Tet truce is approaching.

The Catholic priest from Ha Lan is ambushed at the cut in the pass the morning before Tet.

The survivors say that Viet Cong tried to stop the priest's jeep. They killed the young jeep driver, crashing the jeep. A teenage girl traveling with the priest is wounded. The priest is unharmed but the several hundred thousand Piasters he carries to buy supplies in Ban Me Thuot for Ha Lan's Tet celebration are stolen.

A District truck coming up to the pass behind the jeep hears the shooting. The truck turns and flies back to District blowing its horn as it barrels down the highway. By the time it gets to District, the Ha Lan Popular Force are reporting the ambush on the hamlet radio net.

Using the District 2 1/2-ton and 3/4 ton, Yen moves two Montagnard Popular Force platoons through Ha Lan to the pass. Grabbing a PRC-25 radio, I go with Yen.

The Popular Force from Ha Lan have already left to go up to the pass. Driving up the road, we find them walking up the highway. Dismounting, Yen stays with the District Popular Force, while I walk with the Ha Lan Popular Force.

The Popular Force come on line on both side of the highway and walk up the hill to the ambush site.

The "Viet Cong" have fled.

A couple of small National Liberation Front flags, the size you wave when a bystander at a parade, and an old unexpended "Chi-Com" potato masher grenade are conveniently laying on the ground at the ambush site. The grenade is old and rusted. I doubt anyone would carry it, let alone try to use it.

That afternoon Yen goes to Ban Me Thuot for Tet. After he leaves Captain Hoy orders an operation to Khon Diem, an abandoned hamlet near Con Diem. The attackers supposedly fled in that direction.

Our War

The plan is for the column to sleep that night as close to Khon Diem as it can though still within the artillery fan. Next morning, early, the guns will be moved to Stephanau's plantation; from there they can reach Khon Diem.

Captain Yee is in charge. Popular Force from Ha Lan, the Regional Force company, the Provincial Recon Unit, and two field police, about 120 men, make up the column.

Shortly before dusk we truck to old Buon Ho then walk cross-country to reach a small Montagnard Buon.

There the hamlet chief invites Yee, Bozilov, the Regional Force company commander and me into his long house where we drink nam-pay.

Yee gets plastered. Before leaving he replaces the water in his canteen with nam-pay.

After staying an hour in the Buon, the column starts again towards Khon Diem.

Yee and the Regional Force commander get into an angry argument over where to halt for the evening. Yee wants to bivouac far off the trail that runs between the Montagnard Buon and Khon Diem. The Lieutenant wants to be on the trail to stop anyone warning the Viet Cong. They settle for the trail, the troops flop down and are soon asleep.

At first light, spreading into a line formation, the column walks into Khon Diem's ruins.

Two men break from the bush, running across our front from right to left. The line opens fire and we have a prisoner, the local Viet Cong tax collector. He has a tax receipt book and 5,000 Piasters in a small briefcase. I grab the money.

The column then moves through the remains of the hamlet. A platoon sleeping area is discovered hidden in the trees that line the dry stream bed winding through the hamlet. It looks recently used. Our gunfire may have flushed them. We move cautiously but run into nothing, then head in. The Tet truce begins tonight.

Walking back on the road to old Buon Ho, the column stops at a large Montagnard Buon. Captain Hoy and Duc, the Truong Son sub-chief, are waiting there.

120

The Fight For Rice Continues

Duc grabs the tax collector and starts hitting his face with his fists. Some troops grab Duc and hold him until he calms down.

Then agitated and angry villagers gather around demanding that we hang the tax collector. They recognize him as the Viet Cong who the previous week press-ganged several young men from the Buon. More and more villagers assemble, yelling at Hoy that he turn the tax collector over to them for justice.

The tax collector, haughty and arrogant since his capture, is visibly shaken.

Captain Hoy talks to the people, eventually calming them. We drink some nam-pay and then move the prisoner back to District.

Major Bonds flew in while the operation was on. Major Douglas, our new District advisor, is with him As we drive into the compound both stand in front of our office.

Bonds asks me where I have been. He tells me that he is now acting Province advisor. Lieutenant Colonel Monroe, the Province advisor, is fired.

Monroe supposedly wrote in a report through advisor channels that he could not understand "Why the Vietnamese are so afraid to fight and die as there is nothing in the country worth living for." One of the Vietnamese clerks in the advisor's office gave a copy to the Province chief. The Province chief showed it to Corps.

Monroe flew from Ban Me Thuot to Saigon on the same flight as the Major.

Bonds is upset. We had gone on the operation rather than work on the living quarters. He testily reminds me that working on our quarters is our priority. Douglas calms him down by telling him he will get right on it.

Leaving them, I walk over to Hoy who is a couple of steps away and congratulate him on the operation's success. This is the first Viet Cong taken.

Bonds and the prisoner fly back to Ban Me Thuot.

I did not mention the money to Bonds. After Bonds flies out, the Regional Force Company commander asks me to give him the money taken from the Viet Cong. I

Our War

give him the bulk and the rest to the Ha Lan Popular Force. They will have a happier Tet.

The Regional Force Company uses the money to throw a party. Everyone on the District Headquarters' staff is invited except our new Major. I ask the company commander to invite him but he refuses, saying there is no room.

The company buys and kills a goat with the money. The goat is augmented with bowls of steamy rice with nuc-mam, green vegetables, which look like boiled spinach, and loaves of French bread.

The company commander proudly announces that we will drink "Bambi-Bam" Bier from Saigon. The "Bambi-Bam" is his gift for me. On operations we often discussed the merits of "Bambi-Bam" versus Bier La Rue. As a Saigon native, he thought "Bambi-Bam" far superior. I told him I had never had any and could make no valid comparison. Now I can and do.

The Vietnamese like to drink beer mixed with orange soda; a vile habit. After a few drinks, their faces turn a bright red. Some troops put on a show and the party—held in the administrative hall—lasts late into the night.

During the rest of the week, I get invited to Stephanau's party and another by a retired Vietnamese air force officer who owns a small plantation. It is a good time.

Extend For A Great Deal

CHAPTER TEN

Major Douglas is not the Major. Younger, more interested in the war, an officer who wants to do the job.

He was a recon platoon leader in the Korean war's last days. While trying to roust out guerrillas he had been shot in the leg by his own men and evacuated. Since his wound was the result of friendly fire he did not receive any decorations even the Purple Heart.

He talks about collecting some medals now.

Unlike the Major, Douglas is always pushing Yen to run operations.

He also jumps on the USAID bandwagon, bringing in USAID personnel to give classes to the villagers, particularly farming techniques.

After he gets a look at one of the VISTA volunteers, a good looking, agreeable, blond in her mid-twenties, the team spends time arranging transportation for her to, from and in the District. She is trying to set up home sewing industries, teaching the local women how to use sewing machines.

Without visiting "Donut Dollies" to cheer us all the District advisors welcome her visits though she stays only during daylight.

No one wants the other VISTA workers, a dark, hairy, unwashed female and a couple of longhair males. Rejects from a hippie commune, they spend their time in the Ban Me Thuot bars.

My one concern about Douglas is that as his tour progresses, the pressures start to take their toll. He wakes in the morning with the shakes, then opens his first beer before breakfast to control it. He drinks beer sparingly but constantly the remainder of the day, though never drunk.

Dian gets his transfer to the 173d Airborne and is gone.

Sergeant Nomura, a big placid Papuan, replaces Dian. We soon find out that this placidity is a veneer. Whenever anything happens he speaks fast, loud and incoherently. To get any sense from him, you have to calm him down, then ask specific questions.

Both Stedman and Powers return from Hawaii in love. They had been without a woman for almost a year other than visits with the prostitutes in the Ban Me Thuot hotel. At least Powers used their services. After a military police raid on the hotel I received a Delinquency Report on him for consorting with a prostitute.

They meet two young things upon arriving in Hawaii. With his hormones running amok, Stedman, confusing sex with love, talks about giving up his girl back home and returning to Hawaii. Powers, more pragmatically, just wants to get back to Hawaii.

Both are due to rotate stateside within two months, their one-year tours up.

With their experience, Douglas wants them to stay. He works on them, suggesting they extend their tours for six months. If they do they will receive a thirty-day leave to any place in the states including Hawaii, as well as another R&R in Hawaii.

Stedman is reluctant, saying he will think it over. Powers having no reason to go stateside tells Douglas he probably will extend.

The Rice War Gets Deadly

CHAPTER ELEVEN

Province wants to run a big operation to collect any rice that the Major did not destroy at Con Diem and Khon Diem.

Province and An Loc Regional Force companies, as well as our own, will be used.

The District's 105-MM's will be exchanged for two 155-MM howitzers during the operation. With greater range, the 155-MM's can reach Con Diem from the District compound. Guns will not need to move to old Buon Ho for the operation.

The operation's first day is to take place in the southeast border area between our District and An Loc. The idea is to hit any Viet Cong using the border area as a safe haven. Viet Cong rely on poor cooperation between the Districts to enable units in one to avoid an operation by quickly moving into another.

Our District troops are to block while the soldiers from An Loc and Province push into them.

Early in the morning our troops move by truck, stopping briefly at Ha Lan to pick up a Popular Force soldier as a guide.

Duc, the Truong Son sub-chief, originally was our guide but this morning claims he is too sick to go.

Beyond Ha Lan, we dismount and start cross-country to our objective, a burnt-out hamlet five kilometers away.

With the guide from Ha Lan showing the way, the column after walking four kilometers, crosses a small stream, then takes a steep trail up the far bank moving through thick woods.

The woods end five hundred meters up from the stream. Then the steep path, so sheer in parts that steps are carved in the ground, continues up the hill through a large cleared area.

One scraggly thin tree about three inches in diameter is in the middle of the

Our War

clearing, left of the path.

The column is moving in file, the point almost to the crest, about fifty meters away, not far from our blocking position. Powers, who believes in the combat part of combat medic, is walking as he normally does, near the point.

Stedman carrying the radio and I follow behind the lead platoon. I now start walking rapidly adjacent to the trail up the hill past the troops struggling with their loads. I want to reach the point man by the time he gets to the blocking position.

Suddenly shots sound to our front.

Everyone piles on the ground behind the lone tree.

The Regional Force commander runs pass up the hill, yelling for his troops to spread out and fire. Finally untangling, I grab the radio "mike" from Stedman and start calling in a fire mission.

Just then the firing ceases. Stedman and I run up behind the company commander who is telling the machine gun crew where to set up.

The Viet Cong are gone into thick brush, leaving a trail of broken grass. The imprint where they laid in the grass can be seen. There were five.

I tell the machine gunner to fire in the direction they withdrew. He refuses, not seeing any target.

The wounded point man, a Sergeant and former CIDG, who speaks English, lies nearby shot in the leg. Powers is bandaging him.

Not yet in great pain, the Sergeant laughs at my efforts.

"They will fire only if they see a target," explaining "You never know when you will get more ammunition."

I call a chopper; after an hour plus wait, and several more calls, a Vietnamese flown obsolete H-34 arrives. Vietnamese have last priority for MEDEVAC.

Our column moves late to the blocking position; Province also runs late. It ran into an ambush while moving up Highway 14. A B-40 round hit a jeep killing a soldier.

The Viet Cong knew we were coming.

The Rice War Gets Deadly

After the Province forces pass through, we return to the District.

The next day, Douglas takes the District forces to Con Diem. As they enter the ruins, a fire fight erupts with what looks like Viet Cong work units caught harvesting the rice.

The Viet Cong, keeping up a running fight, withdraw without casualties to the east across a stream.

On the opposite bank, they turn and fight, throwing themselves into pre-dug trenches. These trenches are outside the range of the District 105-MM howitzers. The Viet Cong, however, are in for a surprise; the trenches are well within the range of the 155-MM howitzers.

Douglas calls in a fire mission on the advisor radio; I relay to the guns.

Two salvos and the Viet Cong trenches are bracketed. On the third salvo, the Viet Cong break and run.

Douglas's next fire mission is left 100, up 100. I pass the mission but no fourth salvo is fired. There is a lot of yelling at the guns. Finally, the Province deputy, the Vietnamese Major in charge of the operation, tells me that they cannot swing the guns far enough to the left to fire the mission. They need to move the gun trails.

The Viet Cong are gone by the time the trails are moved and dug in.

Two An Loc companies walking with Douglas cross the stream and report finding blood trails as well as a large intestine. There are no bodies. They also report the troops in contact wore khaki, not the peasant's black pajamas.

Our District soldiers stay in support while An Loc sweeps the woods above the trenches. A Viet Cong work party walks into them and is killed. One An Loc soldier is seriously wounded.

I call Ban Me Thuot requesting a routine MEDEVAC.

American helicopters are available but no Vietnamese.

U.S. Army policy is for the Vietnamese to evacuate Vietnamese wounded.

127

Our War

Even though told the man is dying, the clerks sitting in the rear refuse to send an American helicopter. For two hours I argue for a helicopter. Finally an American helicopter is dispatched after I convince them that the operation forces will not move until the wounded man is evacuated.

The man dies as the helicopter lands.

All MEDEVAC requests now are reported as American.

No rice is found in Con Diem, but the nearby abandoned hamlet of Khon Diem is loaded.

This time trucks from Province are available to move the rice. For two days, trucks move from Ban Me Thuot up Highway 14, then over the dirt track to Khon Diem where they are loaded and returned to Ban Me Thuot.

The rice in Khon Diem is cached in large wooden bins buried in the floors of the destroyed homes. On our operation before Tet the column had walked right by these hidden bins.

After the rice is removed, all the troops return.

Our team throws a party at District for the advisors.

Gerry Brown is getting a reputation as a natural combat leader. But that does not stop everyone teasing him. Unlike most Americans in Vietnam, he has gained weight, putting on 15 pounds eating Vietnamese food. An Loc, like us, is still not paying the surcharge that the MACV mess in Ban Me Thuot wants.

With other advisors from Province and An Loc also there, plans are discussed about pushing the Vietnamese for more joint operations in the border areas.

Powers and Stedman are jubilant. Scheduled to go home soon, they have finally seen real action.

Everyone feels good; the operation was a success.

The Rice War Gets Deadly

Our War

RF company moving by truck. There is always room for one more.

The Rice War Gets Deadly

Weapons captured during an operation at Khon Diem by Province

Our War

CHAPTER TWELVE

A week later the Buon Dlung Canton chief walks into the District compound. After speaking with Yen, he comes to our office. Greatly agitated he starts talking to me.

Though dressed today in the traditional Montagnard male garb, barefoot, in loincloth, with a one-piece pullover shirt, he is the District's leading Montagnard, a member of the National Assembly. Na Han held him in awe.

Educated in France, with a home in Saigon, when in the District he lives in Buon Dlung, a small Buon located near the southern boundary, two kilometers east of Ha Lan. The road to it is a dirt track branching off Highway 14 near the middle of Ha Lan.

I dealt with him often because Buon Dlung was selected as the Montagnard showpiece hamlet for the pacification program.

The Popular Force platoon recruited there was sent to Ban Me Thuot for equipping and training. With that platoon at the training center, two District Popular Force platoons provided security to the Buon.

A schoolteacher, health worker and information worker were also assigned.

Bunkers, palisades and trenches were built.

When the hamlet's Popular Force platoon returned after completing its training, the Canton chief threw a party dedicating the Buon to the "New Life" program. The Province chief attended and a water buffalo blood sacrifice was offered.

Neither the Province chief, who like Lieutenant Thieu, is a Fu Manchu look alike, nor the buffalo killing interested me. They kill the buffalo by hacking it to death with machetes, beginning at its extremities. Blood and gore splatters everywhere. I arrived late, after the buffalo was dead and the Province chief gone.

That day the Canton chief was calm and in control.

Today he is nervous and excitable, speaking so quickly that I cannot understand a word he says. He speaks French with a slight lisp, which in the best of times makes him difficult to understand.

Unable to understand him, I tell him to wait and go and find Lieutenant Long to

Buon Dlung

translate.

Long, translating, tells me that the Canton chief wants a radio to replace the broken AM Motorola radio at Buon Dlung. Each hamlet has these two-way commercial radios. They provide communication at night between the hamlet and the District.

The Canton chief came to me because Captain Yen told him no replacement was available.

Normally poised, even condescending, the Canton's chief nervousness and agitation is odd, particularly for a man who represents Montagnard interests at the national level. After confirming with Yen that there is no other radio available, I calm him down by telling him that I will send Stedman the next day to fix the radio.

That satisfies him and he leaves.

That night, shortly after one, Sergeant Bozilov wakes me yelling that Ha Lan is under attack. Getting up, I hear the distant rumble of sustained gunfire. Dressing, I walk outside across the compound onto a bunker roof on the far side facing Ha Lan.

Green and red tracers ricochet high into the night sky crisscrossing the valley's far end.

Everyone in the compound is up. Yen yells for the Popular Force platoons and Regional Force company to get ready to move. I walk to the Vietnamese communication bunker that is the net control station for the hamlet radio net. Long is there and tells me Ha Lan reports that the attack is on Buon Dlung. They report hearing screams, yells and gunfire.

There are three Popular Force platoons, about 100 men, in Buon Dlung. The two platoons from the District are still there along with the recently returned platoon from Ban Me Thuot. Equipped with carbines and M-1's, all three platoons are well equipped by Popular Force standards. More important, the District platoons contain combat experienced old soldiers, former French army veterans. From the noise they are giving as good as they are getting, though the many green tracers flying in the air indicate a large attacking force.

With the hamlet radio out, there is no contact with the defenders.

We are all standing on the bunker looking at the tracers moving across the sky.

Major Douglas and Captain Yen want to move immediately.

The Regional Force commander refuses to move in the dark unless Province approves. He fears the attack is bait to lure a relieving force into an ambush.

I share his concern.

To resolve the impasse, I tell Stedman to call Province on the advisor radio net, telling them that Yen wants to move but the Regional Force company commander is refusing. Immediately, Province calls Yen on the Vietnamese AM radio net telling him not to move until first light.

There is nothing to do until daylight.

For the next hour the firing dies down then erupts sporadically until eventually it ceases altogether.

I go back to sleep.

Captain Hoy and Lieutenant Thieu are both in Ban Me Thuot. Unknown to us, the Province chief wakes Hoy and orders him to drive back that night to command the relief column to Buon Dlung.

Getting up shortly before five and going outside, I find Hoy returned, driving back that night.

With first light, Hoy leads out the Regional Force company and a Popular Force platoon mounted in trucks to Ha Lan. During the night, Yen had the Popular Force in Buon Trieng secure the road.

After dismounting at Ha Lan, the column is to move overland to Buon Dlung.

Douglas is going with Hoy, taking Powers, Stedman and Nomura. As he leaves I remind him to walk cross-country to Buon Dlung, "Avoid the road." A favorite Viet Cong tactic is to hit a fortified position to draw a relief force into an ambush.

The remaining Popular Force platoons along with Bozilov, Yen and I stay in

Buon Dlung

the compound. I act as radio relay between Stedman with the column and Ban Me Thuot.

The compound FM radio was upgraded. It now has a powerful power pack and ground mounted long antenna enabling us to talk directly to Ban Me Thuot though they cannot hear Stedman's backpacked PRC-25 with short antenna.

Stedman gives routine progress reports.

The column arrives at Ha Lan; it starts to Buon Dlung. Shortly Stedman reports they have reached the Buon. There is no contact. The attackers have withdrawn.

Several minutes elapse, then Stedman screams over the radio that they are receiving fire and pinned down. Heavy firing can be heard in the background. Abruptly his radio goes off, I cannot raise him.

Captain Yen, sitting with me drinking coffee in the "Co-loc-bo" while listening to the FM radio reports jumps up and runs outside.

He yells at Y'Don to get the two remaining platoons in the compound walking to Ha Lan.

Our trucks have not yet returned.

Yen radios the Truong Son at old Buon Ho to walk over and occupy the District to protect the artillery while the Popular Force platoons are gone.

Raising the advisor radio operator at An Loc, I tell him to monitor our net and relay to Province; I will have only a backpack PRC-25. The An Loc operator, closer to us then Ban Me Thuot, can hear our transmissions.

Bozilov and I, with Yen driving, load into Yen's 3/4-ton truck and move out.

The Popular Force platoons file out the gate.

As we move, I tell An Loc to relay to Province that our relief force has been ambushed and request a FAC and MEDEVAC.

The relay at An Loc calls Province, sends my message, then gratuitously adds that we are overreacting. I tell the operator to repeat what I say, not give opinions.

An Army L-19 observation plane from Ban Me Thuot comes up on the net. He is heading our way and will get a FAC up to handle air support.

Our War

Coming down the compound hill I see Sergeant Y'Duc and three other Sergeants standing at the bottom talking outside their huts before they walk up the hill to work (It is still before eight).

As Yen makes the turn onto Highway 14, Y'Duc yells, "What is going on."

With the truck still moving, Yen yells back that the Viet Cong are at Buon Dlung. Y'Duc shouts to stop and wait. Running back to their huts, the Sergeants grab their weapons and returning climb into the 3/4-ton's back.

By now the Popular Force platoons have reached Highway 14 and are walking towards Ha Lan.

As Yen drives down Highway 14, Stedman finally comes back up on the radio.

The gunfire in the background has stopped. Stedman reports that he is now back in the Buon. They were ambushed and ran back into the Buon. Several are wounded; no one knows where Powers is. Others are missing.

The An Loc operator overhears. He reports no helicopters are available; Province will try to get one. Yen, speeding, is now at Ha Lan.

A Ha Lan Popular Force platoon is assembling at the gate that leads to Buon Dlung.

Other Popular Force are putting on their uniforms as they meander in that direction. Yen yells at them to hurry as we drive through the village.

Some Provisional Reconnaissance Unit members, half-naked but armed stand sheepishly, by the gate. They had been asleep in Buon Dlung, fleeing when the attack began. They want to go back to redeem themselves.

An Loc radios a helicopter is on the way to MEDEVAC the wounded.

The chopper pilot comes up on our frequency saying he has a dead Montagnard chief aboard and needs some place to dump the body.

Yen wants to move out.

The advisor jeep as well as the trucks and drivers which moved Hoy and the Regional Force column are still sitting in Ha Lan next to the gate for the trail that goes to

136

Buon Dlung

Buon Dlung. I tell Bozilov to take the vehicles back down the highway and pick up the Popular Force platoons walking to Ha Lan. Also arrange to have the Montagnard chief's body dropped off at the District headquarters and taken care of.

Bozilov is reluctant; he wants to move to the sound of the guns, but does as ordered.

Yen walks through the gate towards Buon Dlung. Some Ha Lan Popular Force, the PRU's, the District Sergeants, some police and a few kids with guns standing around the gate follow him. He tells the Ha Lan Popular Force chief, who is forming his other platoons at the gate, to come after us once he gets the rest assembled.

Leaving the gate, we spread out, come on line and slowly move towards Buon Dlung, walking along a ridge through open rolling terrain parallel to the trail.

Buon Dlung, surrounded by woods, lies on the edge of the great forest that runs east into the mountains separating the highlands from the coastal plains. The Buon Dlung-Ha Lan trail for the first kilometer runs through the cleared fields that surround Ha Lan before entering a tree-covered area that juts out into the fields.

The observation plane is now overhead.

The pilot says men are moving on the Buon Dlung - Ha Lan trail towards the tree line surrounding Buon Dlung.

He is anxious to shoot his rockets. I am just as anxious not to get shot by friendly fire. I tell him that we are in that general area and ask him to describe what he sees.

At this point I have no idea where anyone is other than us. I do not know if he sees us, a platoon from Ha Lan or Viet Cong. Yen has no radio; and though I am carrying a PRC-25, only the advisors are up on that net. My concern is that the troops the pilot sees are the Ha Lan Popular Force or us.

The pilot, though flying right over us, still does not see our line moving separately from the column he reports on the trail.

The pilot answers that the men moving in formation on the road are wearing

Our War

khaki with some kind of helmet on their head. He reports they are now in the woods; he has lost them.

Our force is almost to the tree line.

I run down the line to Yen yelling at the troops on line to "Halt, Halt!" and tell Yen what the pilot said.

From the pilot's description, the men entering the woods are probably Viet Cong. I tell Yen that I think we should stay in the cleared area, moving along the wood's edge. Yen agrees and the troops continue walking along the open ridge, parallel to the trail that has entered the woods on our right. Finally we stop on two small hills and spread out facing the Buon.

From the hilltop, over the trees, I can see the tops of long houses and the Buon's palisades, about 300 meters away.

A FAC is now on station. Though flying overhead he does not see us. Before bringing in air strikes he needs to know where we are to avoid hitting us with friendly fire.

I "pop" a white smoke grenade to mark our position. The FAC does not pick it up.

All I have left is red smoke; I "pop" it.

Jet fighters are now overhead. They see the red smoke, the standard smoke used for marking targets. Luckily the pilots on our net; I overhear them tell the FAC that they see the red smoke marking the target. I do some fast-talking.

The FAC says "Sorry 'bout that" and straightens them out.

The jet fighters have little station time. The FAC wants to put in the strike now.

Stedman told me that they had been ambushed near the small cemetery in the woods by the Buon's main gate. I pass this to the FAC. He picks up the target, fires a rocket marking it—there is a slight pause—then the world in front erupts as the fighters come in, their 20-MM shells exploding in the woods between the Buon and us.

As the planes make their pass, the Ha Lan Popular Force, spread out on the

Buon Dlung

forward slope, get up and drift to the backside. One with an embarrassed smirk on his face walks over and shows me the shrapnel that hit him in the head. Luckily, unlike most Popular Force soldiers, he is wearing a steel pot.

The planes make more passes as we shelter down. You do not see or hear them coming; you know they have fired when the ground in front erupts. After several passes station time runs out and they leave.

Douglas is now on the radio.

"Alpha 5 this is Alpha 6, over."

I respond, "6 this is 5, over."

"6, we are going out. How many do you have, over?"

Standing up and looking around, I count and surprise myself by finding no more then thirty bodies including Yen and myself. "This is 5; about thirty, over."

"6, O.K."-(Long pause) "Stay where you are, we are going out, out."

There is silence for three or four minutes.

Stedman then radios that the troops are walking out the Buon's main gate, coming on line and heading into the cemetery.

Then silence.

Then firing erupts and rises into a crescendo, small arms and explosions.

Stedman screams, "They are throwing grenades."

A long pause, then the Major is on the radio. Excitedly, he yells, "The cowards are running, they won't stand, I can't stop them."

Calling Bozilov on the radio, I tell him to come now with everything—he says he is already moving on the road.

Hunching down, I tell Yen that the Regional Force have broken and run.

Yen stands up, says, "we go," pointing towards the Buon. Waving his arms, yelling at us to follow him, he starts down the hill towards the woods.

In an assault line we start down the open slope. B-40 shells explode among us. The Ha Lan PF stop.

Our War

Yen leading, waves his arm to go on, the pace increases to a jog, the line climbs over a split rail fence inexplicably located on the wood line, and then rushes into the woods.

No one is there.

Rapidly we pass through the woods into a small clearing about 20 meters wide. The Buon's palisade is two hundred meters away at the other end of the clearing. The line spreads into the woods around the clearing and starts for the hamlet. Captain Yen and I walk on the left side.

Stedman reports that the Regional Force company is back in the Buon.

Bozilov radios he is at Ha Lan and moving to Buon Dlung.

The MEDEVAC pilot has dropped the dead chief and radios he is inbound to pick up the wounded.

A Ha Lan PF walking on the right side yells and points towards the ground. Yen and I walk across the clearing.

The Regional Force "Chef de Platoon" is on the ground.

His head rests on a large tree root, his right eye punched out—as if hit over and over there by a hammer. His stomach is crisscrossed with bloody holes. Though still breathing, the sweet smell of death is on him.

A few feet from him is a dead machine gun crew member, face down, his hand still gripping the tripod. He has the same head wound as his Sergeant.

A shout further along the wood line; there is a wounded soldier, gut shot; someone bandaged him.

All weapons and equipment are gone. The Viet Cong were here.

I still have not found Powers.

Two trails intersect where the platoon Sergeant lays. One runs along the clearing to the Buon, the other runs into the woods towards the cemetery. Scuff marks are all over the second trail.

I walk with caution down this trail into the woods. Powers' looted medical bag

Buon Dlung

is on the ground before a bend in the trail. Walking around the bend, Powers lies face down in the trail. No need to look, he is dead.

Next to him, a pair of hob nailed booted feet stick out from a bush. Pushing the brush aside, I find a wounded soldier. Something pierced his helmet, bounced off his head but never penetrated. Knocked out, the Viet Cong left him after taking his weapon and load bearing equipment.

I return to Yen; he sends some PF to bring Powers and the wounded soldier to the clearing.

By now another MEDEVAC is overhead. I direct the pilot to land in the clearing where we are.

The pilot asks if the LZ is clear. I respond yes; we are not receiving fire.

As the chopper comes in, Y'Duc yells that he sees men moving in the woods. Rather than excite the pilot, I do not mention this.

The chopper lands in the clearing; the wounded are loaded. The pilot will not take the dead. He has more wounded to pick up from Major Douglas. The platoon Sergeant, now dead, is left.

Bozilov radios he is moving into the woods on the trail from Ha Lan to Buon Dlung. He has four PF platoons, two from the District and two from Ha Lan.

As the chopper takes off, I run to where Y'Duc is kneeling at the far end of the clearing. Here there is a narrow woods and then another small clearing.

Y'Duc says he saw some men in khaki in the woods on the other side.

Seeing nothing, I take a fragmentation grenade off my web belt, pull its pin and start across the clearing. I intend to throw it into the brush if I draw fire.

Halfway across I have a strange premonition. Looking around I see I am alone. Y Duc and the Popular Force are still in the wood line. I see no one in the woods to my front. Evaluating the situation, I walk back to Y'Duc who is motioning me to hurry.

Bozilov reaches Buon Dlung coming down the main trail from Ha Lan.

I am still carrying the radio. Douglas calls. Hoy wants Yen to move to the Buon

Our War

so we can marry up.

Yen refuses. He wants to stay where we are. The Viet Cong are caught in the forest that juts towards Ha Lan. Our position blocks their withdrawal.

Douglas tells me to put Yen on the radio; Hoy wants to talk to him. I hand Yen the "mike". They ramble, then argue, finally Yen gives the "mike" back saying we are to go to the hamlet taking our dead with us.

Orders are given; tree limbs are torn off to make poles. While getting the branches the PF find a dead Viet Cong. The killing is not all one sided.

Two men carry each pole's end, a body draped over the middle. They look like the Chinese communist moving their wounded that I saw in *TIME* magazine when a child.

We move through the clearing towards a large hole blasted by the Viet Cong in the Buon's wooden palisade.

Entering through the breach, the column walks uphill, through the Buon's center. We pass empty long houses and an unanswered fire arrow with numerous burnt out C-ration cans filled with gas doused rags. It still points fruitlessly in the attack's direction. We reach the main gate on the high ground at the opposite end. Here are the fighting positions, two bunkers and a trench.

All the troops with Douglas are crowded around the bunkers.

As I walk up with Power's body, Douglas comes down the hill.

Stopping the troops carrying the body, he stands there looking down at Power's head, saying nothing. Douglas looks drained.

Still furious at the Vietnamese he turns to me and under his breath says that they are all cowards.

He explains that they had walked out into the cemetery. The Viet Cong let them get close, then threw grenades. Sergeant Thuong, the intelligence Sergeant that shot the FULRO chief, was hit in his finger by a splinter. He started screaming and running towards the Buon. Others started running; Douglas tried to grab them but they ran around

Buon Dlung

him.

Depressingly, he repeats several times "I couldn't stop them; I couldn't stop them."

The dead are laid outside the main gate by a makeshift chopper pad.

The "Chef de Platoon's" Sergeant is by the chopper pad. He stumbles over to his friend's body, tears in his eyes. I can see that the platoon Sergeant is shot in the leg. Douglas tells me he refused to get on the MEDEVAC until the "Chef de Platoon's" body is brought in.

A MEDEVAC comes back to pick up the bodies including a civilian killed the night before.

Douglas still upset, walks over to Powers' body, taking off his field jacket. He covers Power's face. The jacket is lifted into the MEDEVAC with Powers. This futile gesture disturbs me. Powers is beyond needing the jacket, Douglas will; the highlands are cold at night.

The chopper loads and takes off.

As the chopper lifts off, Lieutenant Long and Sergeant Phong drive up in a jeep. They drove through on the same trail that Bozilov came in on; it is clear, no one is there.

Their jeep is loaded with cooked rice, fruit and tins of tea for the soldiers. Not a great meal but under the circumstances welcomed.

Looking around I see Bozilov scrapped the bottom of the District barrel in getting warm bodies into the field. Even Bo-Didly is here, carrying his M-1, wearing a steel pot, which, minus its helmet liner, constantly slips over his eyes. I catch Bo's eye and smile, yelling out "Hi Bo." Bo waves, giving a big grin; then, as the team turns to look, his helmet slips over his face. Everyone laughs.

The FAC, back on station, has more ordnance for delivery.

Soon 250-pound bombs are crashing into the woods, shrapnel hitting around us.

Any returning aircraft with unexpended ordnance from pre planned strikes, no matter what kind, is directed towards the battlefield. Rockets, bombs and cannon fire pound the woods. Finally the FAC announces no more aircraft are on station.

After the air strikes, Long and Phong drive back to the District.

Douglas and Hoy decide to push out again. Bozilov and I line up the PF outside the palisades. The Regional Force company remnants will stay in the Buon.

Bozilov fires shells from his M-79 grenade launcher into the woods while the PF line up. There is no return fire; the woods are quiet.

As the line starts moving, Douglas and Hoy decide they will go with the PF. Yen and I, along with Nomura and Stedman, will stay with the Regional Force company.

Taking the radio off my back, I give it to Douglas.

The PF walk into the woods and soon are lost to sight.

It is a beautiful, sunny day. I go back into the Buon.

Taking off my helmet and web gear I sit in the advisors jeep that Bozilov drove in. Sitting in the front passenger seat, I close my eyes and relax, my feet on the hood, and doze while monitoring the jeep mounted radio.

Bozilov is talking. Douglas must have given the radio to him. They have passed through the woods without contact; it looks like the Viet Cong have left. They are going to turn around and come back.

A few minutes later Bozilov radios that Long and Phong are with him.

While driving back to District Long saw two Viet Cong moving across the fields towards Ha Lan. Chasing them cross-country, they ran them to ground, killing one and capturing the other. They brought the prisoner to Hoy.

Bozilov says the prisoner refuses to talk. He tells me that he will be off the radio for a while.

For a short time there is silence, then Bozilov is back up. These are not Viet Cong but North Vietnamese Army regulars from the 3d battalion, 33d regiment. The two chased by Long were trying to escape the fighting. (Long later tells me that the prisoner at first refused to talk. Bozilov put his pistol next to the prisoner's head. When he

Buon Dlung

continued refusing, Bozilov fired. Then he had Long tell the prisoner the next one would be in his head. The prisoner talked.)

While we wait for Douglas and the PF to sweep back, Stedman and Nomura join me by the jeep and talk about what happened.

They had come cross-country, then entered the woods and reached the Buon.

The Buon Dlung Popular Force were still holding the bunkers and trenches around the main gate.

The Regional Force company then started around the Buon pass the cemetery. Powers was at the head with Nomura while Stedman and Douglas were in the middle.

The lead walked into an ambush. Everybody ran back to the Buon, Nomura never saw Powers after that.

Bozilov calls on the radio. They are now coming back.

Suddenly bullets bounce around us.

Through the widely spaced palisade stakes, I see shadows, then men running at the wood's edge on the Buon's perimeter.

Ducking, everybody dashes to the trench line and bunkers. At the trench I tell Stedman to give me his radio so I can talk to the FAC.

Bozilov reports they did not reach the woods; the fire is too heavy. The PF refuse to move.

The FAC, still overhead, says gunships are on the way.

Major Bonds, our acting Province advisor, now comes overhead in an observation plane. He demands to know why no one greeted him when he landed at District.

I tell him that we are busy.

He stays overhead for about thirty minutes, then leaves. He is flying to Saigon to catch his R&R flight to Hawaii.

Helicopter gunships, with rocket pods and machine-guns, make their pass. As

Our War

they fly above the trees, you can hear the return fire.

Bozilov radios again. A helicopter from Province, bringing water and ammunition has landed at his position. The Province S-2 advisor is aboard. An Loc and Ban Me Thuot Regional Force companies will reinforce us, two companies from each District. Province will run the operation.

The news that we are fighting the North Vietnamese Army has changed attitudes.

The helicopter then drops into the open area behind our trench line. Hovering, the crew chief kicks out water cans and ammunition, then the chopper takes off.

The shooting stops. Leaving the trench, the Regional Force company sits along the backside, their feet dangling into the trench. There is nothing to do until the reinforcements arrive.

Bozilov calls; he tells me to put the Regional Force company's machine gun at the main gate so it fires down the road. It may stop the North Vietnamese moving too freely. The Regional Force company commander, however, wants to keep it in a bunker on the corner of the trench line. The main gate is to the right of the trench line. Eventually, he agrees and a log barrier is built with the gun placed behind it. The gate has been closed since the Popular Force walked into the woods.

The FAC, still overhead, tells me that he is directing any aircraft with unexpended ordnance to the battlefield. The North Vietnamese are under constant attack.

The Ban Me Thuot Regional Force's landing zone is in the open area next to Ha Lan. They, with their advisor, Major Kelly, soon join up with Douglas's force.

The An Loc Regional Force land near Khon Diem, approximately five kilometers cross-country from the Buon. They are to walk to the battle site over the trail that it is believed the North Vietnamese will use to withdraw. It will be some time before they get here.

In the interim, the gunships return.

The North Vietnamese are getting hit hard; their return fire is a lot less.

146

Buon Dlung

A gunship misses its turn point spraying some of the Ha Lan Popular Force. We have five more wounded.

Major Kelly comes up on the advisor net to announce that he and his Ban Me Thuot Regional Force companies are going to attack the woods to their front.

As the attack begins, shells start exploding along our trench line. All of us jump into the trenches. Grabbing the "mike" from Stedman, who is still carrying his radio, I tell Kelly to check fire with their 60-MM mortar.

He replies "Sorry 'bout that."

A crescendo of "pop, pop's" is heard in the distance.

Shells again are exploding on our position.

I yell at Kelly to control his troop's fire, then, abruptly, all firing ceases.

Kelly yells, "The cowards are running from the woods." He radios that he does not understand why they are running and coming back to where he is. Then his voice cracks, he reports seeing wounded.

I realize now that Kelly was not with his troops in the woods but "observing" at the command post. I say something over the radio to him; the berserker in me taking control, I have no idea what. Stedman, when I return the "mike" mentions that he had never seen me that mad.

Douglas now comes on the radio. They will wait for the troops from An Loc before they try again.

The FAC comes up. He has some more ordnance on the way. Dusk is approaching.

The Regional Force company commander leaves the bunker where he, Stedman and Nomura are sitting. Coming over to where I am sitting on the back of the trench, he tells me that if we are not relieved by nightfall he is going to bug out with his people. I tell him there is no need to do that, we can hold on.

For purely personal reasons I am not anxious to crawl around the woods at night. At 6 feet, 190 pounds, it will be hard to pass myself off as Vietnamese.

Our War

Shortly before dusk the Regional Force companies from An Loc arrive at the wood line. They are on the same small hills our column occupied prior to moving into the woods.

The FAC, still overhead, radios he has some napalm coming in. The jelly has a tendency to jump and is impossible to control.

The FAC tells us to get under cover or pull back from the wood line.

The Air Force received bad publicity after making a former West Point football player a hero by dropping some on his troops. They are not interested in making more heroes.

I crawl into the bunker.

The planes, slower, prop driven to insure accuracy, drop their load. The strike is completed as night falls.

The An Loc Regional Force radio that they are in the woods. I go to the main gate to ensure that our soldiers do not fire into them.

It is too dark to see anyone. Gerry Brown radios he is approaching the gate. I can hear the jingle of equipment moving towards us and tell one of the machine gunners to open the gate. Brown and his companies file in.

A fire is started, Brown has LRRP rations that we heat and share.

Artillery fires all night on the routes it is assumed the North Vietnamese are using to withdraw.

All of us are asleep within an hour.

At first light we leave the Buon walking through the woods down the trail to Ha Lan.

Stedman drives the jeep.

The North Vietnamese are gone.

After leaving the woods, Nomura and I get in the jeep and drive to the command post near Ha Lan.

The Province chief is there.

Buon Dlung

They are flying correspondents in to see the battlefield. Caught in the woods jutting out towards Ha Lan, the air strikes massacred the NVA. Over forty-five dead are found in the woods where they made their fight.

The Province chief greets me asking, "Where is Captain Yen?"

Yen left me as soon as we walked from the woods. I assume he returned to District. The Colonel, mad because Yen ignores him, tells me to have Yen report to him.

As I leave the command post, Kelly approaches the jeep asking for a ride to District. I look at him, saying nothing. Kelly steps back, I tell Stedman to drive. I never see Kelly again.

After riding to the District compound, I find Yen in his quarters behind his office and give him the Province chief's message. Yen tells me he has no interest in seeing his boss.

I shave and eat breakfast.

Just as I get comfortable, Province radios that they need an officer to go with the Regional Force companies from Ban Me Thuot. Kelly is returning with his District chief to Ban Me Thuot.

For the next two days I walk with the Ban Me Thuot Regional Force companies pursuing the North Vietnamese Army. A Special Forces "Mike" force kill Viet Cong moving rice at Khon Diem, the only contact. No trace of the North Vietnamese Army is found.

While I am taking my two-day walk in the sun, Captain Yen throws a victory party at Buon Brieng. I know nothing about the party until Douglas radios ordering me to walk to Ha Lan. I leave the American operations Sergeant and RTO from Ban Me Thuot with the Regional Force companies and walk cross-country about two kilometers to Ha Lan. Stedman picks me up in the jeep and drives to Buon Brieng.

Douglas and Yen already have a buzz on.

Yen orders a chicken sacrificed in my honor and several young women put copper bracelets on my wrist.

149

Our War

I ask Yen what the bracelets mean. I have lots, getting them often on our walks when visiting a Buon. Smirking, he explains that it signifies that you are married to the woman who gives it to you, then starts laughing. Lots of nam-pay is drunk.

Towards evening I take the jeep and drive back to Buon Dlung. The Ban Me Thuot Regional Force companies are there waiting for trucks to take them back to Ban Me Thuot. I pick up the operations Sergeant and RTO and bring them to the party. We all drink until late that night.

Though the North Vietnamese Army took a licking, MACV is not happy. Douglas is reprimanded. Division is angry because Powers is the first advisor killed in the division area. They want to know why a medic was killed.

Stedman packs Powers' gear to send to his mother.

Powers owned a plastic, bright red and blue, wind up record player that he bought at the PX. A toy for children, it used no electricity and could be played any time during the day, even when the generators were not on. It often was. The record player plays a special formatted record. The only one Powers had was the record that came with the player, a song by Peter, Paul and Mary asking "where did all the young men go."

The record player always fascinated "Bo." Seeing Stedman packing it, he asks for it. Stedman gives it to him.

Douglas writes Powers' mother a letter saying Powers died a hero. Later, the war generates so many dead that a form letter is developed by the Army to send to the parents; but that is yet to come.

Our new medic, Powers' scheduled replacement, a ten-year veteran E-6, arrives a week after his death.

Powers died a few days before his tour was up.

There is no talk of anyone extending any more.

Buon Dlung

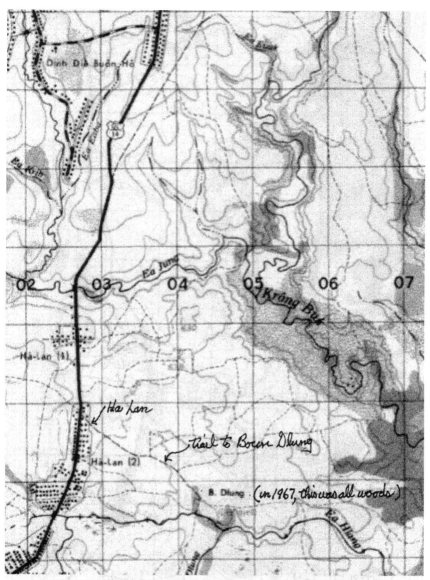

Army Map Service, southern Buon Ho District, (1973 Map)

CHAPTER THIRTEEN

Life continues. Stephanau comes by to offer his condolences. A chaplain from Province arrives and holds a memorial service.

Yen and I visit the wounded in the Ban Me Thuot hospital. It is depressing. The hospital is several long, one-story buildings. Wounded lying on wooden beds stuffed with straw crowd the ward corridors. I leave quickly.

Powers is soon a memory as the living go on with their lives.

Province now bombards us with intelligence reports. The Province S-2 advisor will not come up short again by discounting information. Every rumor is reported. Our local spies also have the fever. They report continuous North Vietnamese Army/Viet Cong battalion size movements in the District.

We also get involved in a new project.

At the compound hill's bottom, on the backside away from Highway 14, is the District's poorest hamlet, Quan Lie. The inhabitants, forcibly resettled by Diem from the coast, have no love for the government or their nearest neighbors, the wealthy resettled Catholics in Ha Lan.

Na Han despised the Quan Lie peasants believing they were Viet Cong supporters.

Besides they constantly complain, mostly about Ha Lan. Ha Lan has the one mill in the District and gets a share of Quan Lie's annual rice harvest as payment for threshing it. Each year's crop is partially mortgaged to Ha Lan to pay off last year's debt. Also as Buddhists they loathe the Ha Lan Catholics.

The hamlet's inhabitants make little effort to maintain the hamlet defenses or even complete the palisade. They tell me they are too weak from lack of food.

For some inexplicable reason, Province decides to make this hamlet our showcase Vietnamese "New Life" hamlet.

The hamlet's Popular Force platoons are shipped to Ban Me Thuot for training

Now There Is Contact

and equipping with new weapons.

With the Popular Force gone, an ARVN company arrives to provide security. A Rural Development Team is also sent into the hamlet.

The team, forty young men and women trained by the CIA in propaganda, organization and military skills based on Viet Cong technique, is to build up an infrastructure loyal to the government. Like the Viet Cong, they wear black pajamas and rubber sandals, and are armed.

While the concept appeals to an academic's theoretical thought process, it ignores reality. Starving peasants in Quan Lie, seeing the wealth of Ha Lan, want their share. Greed and jealousy underlies the simple program pitched to the peasant by the Viet Cong. Supporting the "status quo" does not compete with the Viet Cong's untested promises.

The development team members soon realize they cannot solve the peasant's subsistence existence. They lose their enthusiasm. During the day they can be found hanging around "Howard Johnson's" drinking espresso coffee or cafe-au-lait, watching traffic on Highway 14, dreaming about returning to Saigon. They lack the Viet Cong cadres' fanatical and deadly discipline.

Progress in the hamlet is slow. My daily drive there to see what if any progress is made is consistently disappointing.

The hamlet chief complains that the people are too hungry to do any work on the defenses.

The Viet Cong also organize their own propaganda offensive. The Quan Lie peasants report armed Viet Cong propaganda teams stop them working in the field and harangue them to oppose the government by working slow.

The Viet Cong propaganda line, though, soon changes.

The ARVN company commander reports the peasants now are told that the hamlet is going to be attacked. He is concerned. The Montagnard intelligence net reports rice collecting, ladder building and unit movement.

Our War

While this is going on we get a welcomed new addition. An American radio relay station sets up in the compound.

The team, a Sergeant with three other enlisted men, gives us a serious increase in fire power and mobility. The four-member-team carries an M-60 machine gun, automatic firing M-16's and a M-79 grenade launcher. They also has two 2 1/2-ton trucks. One mounts the "hooch" containing their radio equipment. We borrow the other to move troops.

Their addition to our mess adds four new mouths to feed, justifying "Bo" introducing his nephew as assistant cook. The nephew immediately hires a Popular Force soldier to do the more menial tasks like washing dishes or clothes.

"Bo" has reached managerial status, giving orders and supervising his staff; he spends his sizable free time traveling to Ban Me Thuot where a dentist is replacing his teeth with gold caps. After each visit he walks around the compound flashing a huge grin so everyone can see his golden teeth.

A chopper from division lands at the compound a few days after the radio relay team arrives.

James Garner, a television actor, is making a morale tour visiting troops. He stays with us for the day, the chopper picking him up in the evening. I had not watched television in years and did not know who he was. But Douglas and everyone else know him. Douglas takes him into the "Co-loc-bo" and he spends the day with the team talking and drinking beer. He is good company; the troops enjoy his visit.

With the reports that the Viet Cong are about to attack Quan Lie, Douglas decides to lead an operation to a Buon in the north, near the artillery fan's limit. It is not far from where the ARVN battalion was ambushed several months earlier. The Buon sits on an east-west trail that runs parallel to the road that goes to old Buon Ho.

For several weeks our spies report that the Viet Cong move through the Buon during daylight hours.

Now There Is Contact

Douglas takes two radio relay crew members who have been begging to go on an operation. They carry their M-60 machine gun.

Going out, the operation is without incident.

Walking back Captain Yee at the column head flushes a wild pig in the bush. He shoots it. The long winding column, thinking it is under attack, opens fire; so does the M-60 machine gunner. The pig is very dead. The radio relay men very scared.

The world crashes around us shortly after one the next morning. Jumping from my bunk, I run from the "Co-loc-bo," to see a star spangled sight of shells bursting in the air.

Luckily the mortar shells are landing short, outside the camp's barbed wire.

The mortars are firing from the backside of Quan Lie where the Viet Cong propaganda teams operated. The teams were a ruse to distract attention from the Viet Cong doing the site surveys for the real target—the advisors.

Some one fingered us.

The thirty rounds fired are on line but fifty yards short of the "Co-loc-bo." The gunners failed to adjust correctly for the height difference between their firing position and the compound hill.

The next morning, the Buon Brieng Montagnard village chief walks in. He reports that Viet Cong carrying mortars came through the Buon Douglas's column was at shortly after Douglas left.

Yen is relieved for not showing respect to the Province chief after Buon Dlung, as well as getting an American killed, and for any other reason that the Province chief can think up. Yen is a brave old soldier, but no politician.

Hoy is now District chief.

With increasing Viet Cong activity in the artillery fan, Douglas pushes him for more patrols.

Stephanau comes by one evening reporting that Viet Cong are on his plantation. His workers tell him that a propaganda team is there during daylight hours, haranguing them. He is upset because he is not getting a full days work.

Douglas gets Hoy to run sweeps through the plantation to try and pick up the propaganda team.

The sweeps are walks in the sun, coming up empty.

With the plantation within a few kilometers of the District compound, only two advisors go on each walk.

Eventually my turn comes to take the walk. I take Maddy our new RTO to break him in. Formerly at Ban Me Thuot District, he was the RTO that walked with me and the Ban Me Thuot Regional Force company after Buon Dlung. He volunteered to replace Stedman who rotated. He hopes to see some action with us.

We are walking with the Regional Force company and two Ha Lan Popular Force platoons.

This morning the Regional Force company moves listlessly. Given typhus shots early that morning, they are not too happy going out.

The plan is to go to the plantation's northern perimeter, then sweep south through the plantation.

To reach the northern edge the column walks north on Highway 14 then cross-country to the river from which the hamlets along Highway 14 draw their water.

Spanning the river is a flimsy bridge made from several thin logs suspended between two others logs stuck into the ground on each riverbank.

The river is not deep.

I decide not to chance my weight on the bridge, wadding across, the first to the other side.

The rest of the column will take time getting across as one or two men can be on the bridge at a time.

I have to take a shit after crossing the stream. A small hill with trees and bushes is to the trail's left. I climb it to get some privacy and relieve myself.

Now There Is Contact

Looking around I notice two dark figures moving about four hundred meters away on a trail parallel to ours. The area between the trails is open; overgrown with low brush about waist high.

The figures look like Montagnard women. They wear dark clothing and carry split bamboo baskets on their back.

The hill I am on blocks the bridge and the troops crossing from their view. But they cease walking and look in my direction towards the bridge.

The soldiers are making a racket laughing and joking as they cross. A half-mile from the District headquarters, in broad daylight, no one is concerned about security.

Then one of the dark figures turns sideways. With the change in profile, I sense that what I thought was a small stick is a carbine butt. The bamboo baskets are canvas backpacks.

After pausing and listening the figures now start moving rapidly away from me. Raising my carbine, I fire. After old Dat Hieu, I placed tracers every couple of rounds to track where my rounds go. Guiding on the tracers I spray the area as the figures dive for cover.

Hearing the shooting, the Regional Force company runs up.

I explain what happened, pointing out where the Viet Cong are. A Sergeant forms his squad on line and sweeps across the valley floor pass the Viet Cong position. The squad then comes back on line through where the Viet Cong were last seen.

The Sergeant waves us down, there are blood trails. Both Viet Cong are hit.

The column splits up, each follows a trail.

Our man moves for a couple of hundred meters cross-country, then into dense brush.

On hands and knees the company commander crawls into the brush. Maddy and I follow.

Some Ha Lan PF also move into the brush. It is thick, I cannot see anything.

Suddenly a PF crawling in the brush next to me gives a piercing scream.

Our War

The company commander jumps back into me; I fall back into Maddy; we all bound from the brush as the yelling stops. I cannot see the Viet Cong but the Ha Lan PF is standing on the clearing's edge yelling at him. The Viet Cong is yelling back. I finger a grenade.

Then the PF jumps into the brush and pulls the Viet Cong out. Maddy and I were inches from the Viet Cong's hiding place when the Popular Force soldier yelled. Thankfully the Viet Cong elected not to fire his carbine and be a dead hero.

After this Maddy who has only his .45 pistol, not wanting to carry both a carbine and the radio, carries his carbine.

The Viet Cong is tall for a Vietnamese, almost my size. Several of my bullets had hit him in the leg. The carbine's low velocity bullets, fired at long range, barely broke his skin; he will be fine in a few days.

His capture is a great relief to me. Firing on instinct, I was not sure if I had shot Viet Cong or Montagnard women.

Maddy radios for a helicopter.

The other Viet Cong gets away.

A couple of days later intelligence reports that the Viet Cong captured is their assistant District chief. I feel good; I shot and captured my Viet Cong counterpart.

Douglas tells me to write up a recommendation for a medal. I refuse, embarrassed to write that I shot them while taking a shit; besides writing yourself up for a medal is contemptible.

Viet Cong activity continues.

The Recon company from the division runs a small operation around Con Diem borrowing Nomura. Setting up on the trails to the east, they kill several North Vietnamese Army soldiers who wonder down the trails in broad daylight singly or in small groups.

Reports continue of a North Vietnamese Army battalion in that area.

Province continues to report large enemy units in the District. They are treated with skepticism. Most are unbelievable, particularly troop movements.

Now There Is Contact

Sources are not reliable. Even after something happens, and we get a story, I wonder if it is not fed to us to move us in the wrong direction.

The constant reports, however, understandably upset our new medic. After all he replaced a dead man.

Our new medic, in his early thirties, not particularly bright, is a careerist who joined the army because the pay is regular and secure, not for fun, travel and adventure.

One morning he is not around for breakfast nor can we find him in the compound.

The initial building and bunker search is futile. Finally, after several hours, the Vietnamese discover him hiding deep in the tunnel complex that runs under the compound.

He cowers in the tunnel holding his head, telling Douglas he has a "toothache".

Maddy calls Province for a MEDEVAC, a chopper arrives and shortly our new medic is on his way. No one expects to see him again.

Four days later, a chopper lands and our medic gets off smiling, saying a dentist at Nah Trang fixed his "toothache."

Several days after our medic's return our late night is disturbed by a number of loud explosions in the direction of old Buon Ho.

Standing on a corner bunker, I see red and green tracers intersecting against the black moonless sky.

The old Buon Ho radio operator reports that it is under attack with mortars and small arms fire, the camp commander killed in the first salvo.

Yen, before leaving, had sent Sergeant Y'Duc to be the commander. I feel miserable.

Using our AM radio, Maddy raises Ban Me Thuot requesting air support. He asks they come up on the FM net. Our jeep, with its mounted FM radio, is moved next to

Our War

the corner bunker. The loudspeaker is turned to full volume so transmissions can be heard while standing on the bunker.

Within minutes, gunships are up on the net, coming up Highway 14 from Ban Me Thuot.

The sky is pitch black; nothing other than the fireworks at old Buon Ho can be seen.

As the choppers come up the highway, the firing ceases. Everything is dark. Douglas radios the lead chopper pilot that old Buon Ho is under attack.

The lead pilot responds he knows the target. I can hear the gunships but not see them. The pilot says he is going to start his target run.

Douglas, and the compound staff gather on the bunker's top to watch the fire works.

As the choppers begin their run, I realize that the choppers are getting louder, not receding, as they should if heading towards old Buon Ho.

Jumping off the bunker, I run to the jeep, turn its lights on, yelling on the jeep radio to the lead pilot that if he sees lights on the target he has the wrong one.

"Sorry 'bout that," says the pilot as he moves off in the new direction that I give him with specificity.

Soon they are over old Buon Ho. The pilot reports oilcans are burning in the corners of the compound to mark it, while a fire arrow points in the direction of the attack. The pass does some good as heavy ground fire is directed at the gunships. Red and green tracers light up the sky.

A C-47 is now overhead. An obsolete slow moving World War II cargo plane, "Puff the Magic Dragon" is equipped with flares and Vulcan machine guns, mini-guns capable of putting out a huge spiral of bullets in seconds. It sounds like a sick cow when it fires, giving off a long "Moo."

The helicopters now out of station time head in to refuel.

"Puff" will be able to stay on station for several hours.

Now There Is Contact

"Puff" lights the area with flares; then begins making passes, firing. At first the attackers fire back, then after several passes, there is no return fire.

At first light, a helicopter from Ban Me Thuot takes Bozilov and our medic to old Buon Ho.

I am angry. Douglas refuses to allow me to go, telling me that he needs me to handle the relief efforts from our compound.

Hoy, overcautious after Buon Dlung, takes till noon to clear the road before moving a relief force overland.

The Truong Son "Chef de Camp" and his family are the only dead. It is he not Y'Duc who died.

The first mortar salvo landed on the "Chef de Camp's" thatched hut in the compound's center next to the flagpole. His wife and four children also died in their beds during those first seconds.

We find no Viet Cong casualties. Spent rounds and indentations where they laid in the brush are the only indications that they were there. There is no pursuit.

Two Popular Force soldiers walk in while we are there. They were the listening post outside the compound last night.

They fell asleep. Viet Cong were all around when they woke up. They took off their uniforms, abandoned their weapons and fled deeper into the brush. Some armies would have shot them for dereliction of duty; not this one.

With all the enemy activity reports in the District, the Special Forces at Buon Bleck want to run an operation in our operational area. Their Captain drives to District and tells us he is going to go into the area northeast of Con Diem.

Since they will be outside our artillery fan the discussion turns to how the Special Forces unit will get artillery and air support. Conventional military wisdom dictates that you keep within an artillery fan, or at least have dedicated air support. These give you the edge in any fight.

Our War

Douglas tells the Captain that there could be a North Vietnamese Army regiment in that area. Our intelligence indicates that at least a North Vietnamese Army battalion is using it as a base area. They had mortared us twice and attacked Buon Dlung. Douglas recommends that the Special Forces use pre planned air since outside our artillery fan.

The Captain scoffs at the warning. He has been successful operating without artillery or air cover in the north. Giving us his FM frequency, he does ask Douglas to monitor it "just in case." The next day, taking two CIDG companies, he goes in, leaving Highway 14, walking overland.

Two days later, the Buon Brieng village chief walks in with intelligence that he saw a North Vietnamese Army unit operating in the Special Forces target area. We pass this information to the Special Forces Captain.

He radios back that he is not worried; he can handle anything that comes his way.

We continue to monitor. The third day, shortly before noon, the Captain radios they are moving into a Buon north of Con Diem. Then he reports hearing shooting. A few seconds later his Lieutenant is on the radio, sobbing, yelling that the situation is desperate; ambushed, the Captain is wounded, his jaw shot away.

A FAC is immediately overhead The FAC had landed at the compound airstrip the first day of the Special Forces operation. Douglas convinced him to stay on station because he thought the Special Forces unit too exposed. The FAC soon has planes on target.

A "MIKE" force out of Pleiku—Special Forces units designated to react to emergencies—is flown in. The ambushing NVA unit escapes.

Now There Is Contact

Y'Non, or "Bo," our "major domo."

Our War

Montagnard woman and children moving on a trail.

Now There Is Contact

Approaching a Montagnard Buon.

Our War

CHAPTER FOURTEEN

There are no Popular Force units in Buon Ho hamlet, the business district located at the bottom of the compound hill. Hamlet Youth, a paramilitary organization, provide security. This is the original organization that eventually evolved into the Popular Force units.

The Village chief controls the Hamlet Youth. Its members have no military obligation, do not train, nor receive pay. They are poorly armed with cast off weapons, French Labelle's, shotguns and World War II German submachine guns.

A few nights after the Special Forces action heavy firing is heard from the village.

The Village chief reports on the hamlet radio net that Viet Cong attacked a Hamlet Youth patrol. There is one dead and one wounded.

Hoy tells him to bring the wounded man to the District. A MEDEVAC is called.

Soon Joe the village chief drives his jeep up the hill; the wounded man lying across the back on a board.

Placing the wounded man on our kitchen table, our medic works on him, giving him an IV, morphine and bandaging his wounds.

An area outside the compound gate is lit up using Jeep lights for the MEDEVAC to land. It soon arrives.

To my mind this is all there is to the incident, another contact with people shot.

Two weeks later, though, Hoy has the village chief hog-tied on the ground in front of the police station, keeping him there all day. At night he puts Joe in the bunker jail but unusual for a prisoner, puts an armed guard there.

Joe, the name I know the village chief by, and the one he responds to, is in his late thirties. Someone told me he had been an ARVN NCO. After discharge he started a vehicle repair shop and operates a garage at the junction of Highway 14 and the dirt road to old Buon Ho. He repairs our jeep when needed.

The Americans are Here

A friendly outgoing guy, he acts more American then Vietnamese; the advisors think him a bright, hard working man who is the type Vietnam needs.

Na Han appointed him Buon Ho Village chief, the most important village.

Watching Joe thrust up, I initially think Hoy is trying to show up the advisors. Joe, the friend of the American advisors, our protégé, a working class man who in the best American tradition worked his way to a powerful position in the District, cannot be bad.

I feel it is a ploy by Hoy to discredit the advisors.

Lieutenant Long tries to correct my idea that Joe's arrest was aimed at the advisors. He tells me that Joe has "done very bad things," so bad in fact that he cannot tell me what it is.

The day after my conversation with Long, I see Stephanau go into the police station, an unusual step since he tries to avoid the local gendarmes.

Answering my question as to why he went there, Stephanau explains that Joe and the Hamlet Youth stole coffee from his plantation and sold it in Ha Lan.

Stephanau found coffee bags from his plantation in Ha Lan. He told the police and they were investigating when the Hamlet Youth were shot.

The men shot, though not the thieves, knew about it. Joe, Mafia style, ambushed them to eliminate witnesses. Unfortunately for Joe, the wounded man, though not seeing who shot him, has a fair idea who did it and why.

Joe looks forlorn; everyone ignores him. Soon he is gone to Ban Me Thuot for trial.

Long, who is my source for local gossip, also provides some other discouraging news. Duc, the Truong Son sub-chief, is a suspected Viet Cong agent.

They suspect him because he said he was sick and did not go as our guide on the day we walked into the ambush. Long, Duc's friend, tells me he thinks Duc works for the Viet Cong because they kidnapped his father.

With our little world being turned upside down, I even begin to wonder about

Our War

Long, particularly in light of his family's Viet Minh background. It is easy to become too paranoid.

Hoy wants to run a small operation out to Con Diem. Douglas, the other advisors, and Captain Yee will go with the troops.

With the compounds 105-MM's replaced with 155's, the guns need to be moved only to Stephanau's plantation to give the necessary range.

Hoy and I, Douglas still refusing to let me go on operations, will stay with the guns parked in the large field between Stephanau's house and the huts that his workers live in. The field is normally used as a soccer field and for other events at the plantation and village.

Other than some Popular Force soldiers, no one remains at the District compound.

Shortly after the guns are parked, Stephanau comes down and invites me to lunch. Rotating in two days, my tour of duty over, it will be my last time to see him.

It is another beautiful, sunny day. Nothing is happening.

Shortly before noon, an unfamiliar American voice comes up on the advisor net requesting permission to land at the District. I reply that there is no one at District and describe my location.

A helicopter whips around the trees and touches down.

I am sitting in the jeep, smoking my pipe, reading a novel while monitoring the radios; helmet less, wearing worn, washed out, wrinkled fatigues, carrying neither weapon nor wearing load bearing equipment, all of which is thrown in the jeeps back seat. I am securely surrounded by several Popular Force platoons.

As the helicopter touches down, a Captain in new, starched, pressed jungle fatigues, steel pot with camouflage cover, spit shined jungle boots, and newly issued complete load bearing equipment, carrying a M-16, jumps out and runs toward the jeep.

Getting out of the jeep, I start towards the helicopter. The helicopter surprises me by taking off, doing a "touch and go."

The Americans are Here

The chopper immediately hits the electrical power line running to the workers hut from the generator by Stephanau's house; the broken wire wraps around the rotor.

The pilot manages to land in the spot he lifted from.

By this time the man running reaches me, identifying himself as a battalion S-2 in the 4th Infantry Division.

He tells me that the battalion is operating in the District north of Con Diem.

Now with the chopper staying, the Lieutenant Colonel battalion commander walks over accompanied by an American correspondent traveling on the helicopter. The correspondent is a balding, middle aged chubby from some paper in Kansas.

They will have to wait for parts to be flown in to make repairs.

The damage done to Stephanau's workers property upsets me. To help smooth over the situation, I suggest we walk up to Stephanau's house and have lunch. The correspondent goes ballistic, stridently condemning the French, saying they all work for the Viet Cong.

The Colonel gets the message, declining.

I am pissed; excusing myself I drive up to Stephanau, apologize for the damage done by the chopper telling him that I will not be coming to lunch, then return to the Americans.

Using my map, the Colonel points out where his units are. His units are on the trail that the Special Forces had used to approach Con Diem eight months previously. I tell him that the Special Forces had run into a Viet Cong camp there; the District also had the same report. His units do not find it.

I voice my concern that his units may run into our soldiers operating at Con Diem. I ask why he did not coordinate with us.

The battalion commander tells me that they had met with the Province advisors but asked Province not to tell the Vietnamese or us that they were coming into the District. He was afraid that the Viet Cong would get that information.

The battalion commander wants to use some District police and Popular Force

Our War

soldiers to search traffic on Highway 14.

Hoy is standing with me and I introduce them.

They agree that in two days District will provide some Popular Force soldiers and police to go on a helicopter assault to Con Diem.

The helicopter is soon repaired; the Americans with their starched fatigues, shined combat boots and marvelous equipment load and fly away.

Gerry Brown is shot dead.

His Regional Force company was sniped at from a wood covered hill when returning to An Loc from an operation. Brown ran up the hill at the sniper; he was shot once in the head and killed instantly, the only casualty.

The following day a helicopter takes me and my duffel bag to Ban Me Thuot. There the mail run flies me to Nah Trang where I hitch another ride to Saigon.

At Saigon, I again stay at Koepler compound.

The clerks there are surprised to see me.

My MACV records are gone. Another Captain with my name, though different middle initial, had been killed. Eventually I convince them I am alive and get a flight out.

Nomura comes by. He is in Saigon to pick up the movie projector that goes with the cinemascope lens received a year ago. Special Services finally has it.

He tells me that the day after I left the Americans came as planned.

Of course the Popular Force soldiers were not ready—time in seconds and minutes is not critical—it is not part of their life.

The American Colonel went into a rage—his schedule was off.

Laughing at the Americans, we shake hands and say good-bye.

The Americans are Here

Bunker used as jail

ADDENDUM

Captain Chris C. Vurlumis was killed in action on June 8, 1966.

Specialist Fifth William Maxwell Powers was killed in action on February 22, 1967.

Captain Gerald Austin Brown was killed in action on May 16, 1967.

Master Sergeant Don Faurot Dian was killed in action with the 101st Airborne Division on April 23, 1968.

Their names are engraved on our nation's black wall.

Made in the USA
Middletown, DE
29 March 2023

27869759R00104